Fiction against history
SCOTT AS STORYTELLER

While Walter Scott was acutely conscious of the fictionality of his narratives, his readers have too often missed his cues. Assuming Scott's keen awareness of the problems of historical representation, James Kerr reads the Waverley novels as a grand fictional project constructed around the relationship between the language of fiction and historical reality. Scott deliberately played fiction and history off against one another, not only as artifice against reality, but as codified forms of written discourse. For Scott, fiction and history are verbal worlds, forms of understanding that appear at one moment radically different, at another virtually indistinguishable. Despite his deliberation, we can see throughout Scott's novels a tension between the romancer, recasting the events of the past in accordance with recognizably literary logics, attempting to fool the credulous reader with his illusions of the past, and the historian, presenting an accurate account of the past, faithfully depicting things as they were. This contradiction, reflected in the generic mixture of romance and realism that runs through the novels, remains unresolved, even in the most self-conscious of his works. It is in this interplay of fiction and history that the complexity of the Waverley novels is to be found.

Fiction against history

SCOTT AS STORYTELLER

JAMES KERR

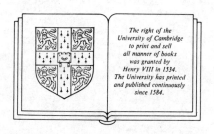

The right of the
University of Cambridge
to print and sell
all manner of books
was granted by
Henry VIII in 1534.
The University has printed
and published continuously
since 1584.

CAMBRIDGE UNIVERSITY PRESS

Cambridge

New York   New Rochelle

Melbourne   Sydney

K835531

Published by the Press Syndicate of the University of Cambridge
The Pitt Building, Trumpington Street, Cambridge CB2 1RP
32 East 57th Street, New York, NY 10022, USA
10 Stamford Road, Oakleigh, Melbourne 3166, Australia

First published 1989

Printed in Great Britain at
the University Press, Cambridge

British Library cataloguing in publication data
Kerr, James
Fiction against history; Scott as
storyteller
1. Fiction in English. Scott, Sir Walter,
1771–1832
Waverley novels – Critical studies I. Title
823'.7

Library of Congress cataloguing in publication data
Kerr, James, 1953–
Fiction against history.
Includes index.
1. Scott, Walter, Sir, 1771–1832 – Criticism and
interpretation. 2. Historical fiction, Scottish –
History and criticism. 3. Scotland in literature.
I. Title.
PR5434.H5K47 1989 823'.7 88–30511

ISBN 0 521 36425 6

WS

To the memory of my
mother and my father

CONTENTS

ACKNOWLEDGEMENTS

I would like to thank John Richetti, who first encouraged me to write about Scott and who has followed this project patiently from its inception to its present form. I am grateful to George Levine, for his invaluable advice and his enthusiasm for the "Author of Waverley." I owe special thanks to Barry Qualls, for his friendship and for his criticism. His support has helped me bring this project to fruition, and his challenges have made this a better book.

I would like to thank Kevin Taylor of Cambridge University Press for guiding me through the process of revision. I would also like to thank the editors of *ELH*, *Studies in the Novel*, and *Texas Studies in Literature and Language*, where earlier versions of my work on *The Heart of Midlothian*, *The Bride of Lammermoor*, and *Redgauntlet* were published.

A NOTE ON CITATIONS OF
THE WAVERLEY NOVELS

In citing passages from the Waverley novels, I use *The Edinburgh Waverley*, 48 vols. (Edinburgh: T. and A. Constable, 1901–03). I have checked all passages cited against the "Magnum Opus" Edition, 48 vols. (Edinburgh: Cadell, 1829–33), and have found no significant variants.

1

THE HISTORICAL NOVEL AND THE PRODUCTION OF THE PAST

My subject is Walter Scott the storyteller, the romancer who forged illusions of the past from an admixture of literary form and historical record, and the historian who used the logics of literary form as instruments for understanding the past. Storyteller and historiographer, Scott constructed his fictional project around the relationship between the language of fiction and historical reality, the possibility of grasping the movements of history in the language of fiction, and the denial of that possibility. Conscious of the fictionality of his narratives, he deliberately played fiction and history off against one another, not only as "artifice" against "reality," but as codified forms of written discourse. "Fiction" and "history" are verbal worlds for Scott, forms of understanding that appear at one moment radically disparate, at another virtually indistinguishable. This is where the complexity of the Waverley novels is to be sought, in the interaction of fiction and history.

In the Waverley novels, the mixed genre of historical romance becomes a field in which perceived contradictions in history can be recreated and resolved. It is a zone of freedom, a verbal realm apart from history, the limits of which are prescribed by the taleteller's imagination, where the ugly facts history throws in the way of the writer can be made into appealing, or at least consoling, stories about the past. For Scott, the facts of the past are the stuff of tales. Yet they serve not only as the raw material of his fiction, but as its justification as well. What made the Waverley novels so popular in Scott's own time, and what still appeals to many contemporary readers, is the sheer elaborateness of the worlds Scott created in his novels. But this density of realistic detail serves also as a pretext for writing romances. Scott's visions of social harmony require the endorsement of actuality lent to them by his realism. He uses the facts of the past both to ratify and to undermine the force of his romance plots. History becomes at once his alibi and his enemy. The historical romancer not only combines romance with "reality," but, viewing history as simply another way of seeing things that is at odds with the perspective of romance, writes history anew.

While Scott was manifestly conscious of the artificial nature of his work, some of his more reputable admirers have missed his cues. We know that in Scott's own time, the popularity of the Waverley novels rested largely on the perceived reality of his writing.[1] Scott is best known to contemporary readers as the inventor of the historical novel, a figure whose most significant contribution to the genre rests in his attempts to portray great historical movements. Due in no small part to the work of Georg Lukács the notion of Scott as an accurate depictor of the past has remained a significant issue among Scott's interpreters. The Scott created by Lukács is the instigating genius of a new genre, the originating consciousness of historical realism, faithfully portraying the crucial social and political changes of British history.[2] But the claims made for Scott's historical veracity, even by a reader of Lukács's philosophical sophistication, assume the possibility of a direct and spontaneous relation between word and world, between the language of fiction and historical reality. A novel may deal with real history, and it may even be empirically accurate in its details. But it remains a fictive treatment of history, as Terry Eagleton has expressed it, "an operation on historical data according to the laws of textual production":[3]

History ... operates upon the text by an ideological determination which within the text itself privileges ideology as a dominant structure determining its own imaginary or "pseudo" history. This "pseudo" or "textual" real is not related to the historical real as an imaginary transposition of it. Rather than "imaginatively transposing" the real, the literary work is a production of certain produced representations of the real into an imaginary object. If it distantiates history, it is not because it transmutes it into fantasy, shifting from one ontological gear to another, but because the significations it works into fiction are already representations of reality rather than reality itself.[4]

History enters the novel, but only in retextualized form, only as ideology.[5] The real is visible in the novel only in its effects, in the transformations worked upon it by the forces of literary production. Despite any overt claims it makes to representing history, the novel is an evasion of history, an attempt to create a safe zone of language in which the forces of the real can be contained and managed. Even the classical historical novel has as its object not history, but ideology. Even in fiction that conceives of history as its subject, history can be present only as a "double-absence,"[6] as a production of a production of the real. History is available to us only in the gaps and fissures that appear in the surface of the novel, in the formal disjunctions and thematic oppositions visible in so much of Scott's writing. The Waverley novels would seem to approach the real more closely than the work of Scott's Gothic predecessors. What that means is simply that the "reality-effect" is stronger there, that Scott's fictional method serves to emphasize the "pseudo-real" to a greater degree than the techniques of the writers labelled as Gothics. Scott's version of the Jacobite rebellion in *Waverley* signifies not the real struggles between the British government and its rebellious subjects, but the ways in which early-nineteenth-century Britain represented itself in fiction. While Scott's pictures of the past contain elements of the real, they are, inescapably, ideological.

But Scott's work is never simply identical with ideology. It is a work of transformation upon ideology, a self-conscious production of produced representations of the past. Scott's novels are fictive reconstructions of a historical subtext of which English colonialism is a central pattern. His immediate historical subject in *Waverley* is the Jacobite rebellion of the mid-eighteenth century. The larger historical subtext of the novel is the anglicization of Scotland, the process of political and cultural assimilation Scott attempted to analyze in *The Heart of Midlothian* (1818). We must bear in mind that the anglicization of Scotland is more than an issue in regional history, a minor disagreement between Britons. It is a version, writ small, of a larger pattern of exploitation, a movement central to England's relationship with Ireland and Wales, which would occur on a much greater geographical and economic scale in India and Africa. To borrow the phrasing of a recent social-historical account, the deeper historical subtext of the novel is the process of "internal colonialism."[7] While Scott could not have conceived of himself as an agent of "internal colonialism," at some level he knew what he was writing against. His novels are fictions written to defer the effects of history, deceptively casual efforts to contain the forces of history by means of story, to alter the past he has evoked.

In the early novels of rebellion, Scott takes a traumatic moment from the textual records of British history and attempts to assimilate it to a formal pattern that he has knowingly drawn, or, as Northrop Frye would say, "kidnapped," from the literary world of romance.[8] The effect of this transgression, a crime openly repeated across the Waverley endings, is to shift potentially threatening material from one generic realm, one mode of emplotment, to another.

By this crossing of generic boundaries, Scott accomplishes the "reemplotment" that Hayden White regards as one of the fundamental ideological motives of historical writing. White's historian is as much an inventor as a discoverer of the past. More artificer than scientist, he approaches the historical record with a notion of the kinds of configurations that can be recognized as stories by his audience. He brings to the record a set of preconceptions, shared with his audience, about how a particular kind of event – the Jacobite rebellion of 1745 or the Cameronian revolt of 1679 – might be emplotted. The form of the historian's account depends on his emphasizing of certain elements and his repression of others. This is essentially a literary, story-making activity: a set of events is not a story in itself, but merely a set of possible story elements subject to the historian's procedures of selection.

White compares the activity of the historian to the work of the therapist in psychoanalysis:

The therapist's problem ... is not to hold up before the patient the "real facts" of the matter, the "truth" as against the fantasy that obsesses him ... The problem is to get the patient to re-emplot his whole life history in such a way as to change the meaning of those events for him and their significance for the economy of the whole set of events that make up his life.

The events in the patient's past that have brought about his symptoms are "detraumatized by being removed from the plot-structure in which they have a dominant place and inserted in another in which they have a subordinate or simply ordinary function as elements of a life shared with all other men." The historian's task is to place "traumatic" or threatening events within the configuration of a recognizable and reassuring story. The historian seeks to "refamiliarize" his audience with events that have been forgotten or repressed, to bring those events to consciousness and to situate them within the form of a familiar plot.[9]

The motive of Scott's kidnapping is no less than the reemplotment of a historical crisis. In *Waverley*, he removes the Jacobite rebellion of 1745 from the historical narrative of dynastic politics in which it occupies a central position and sets it in the romance plot of the hero's career, in which it can have only a subordinate role. By means of this simple shift, the event is transformed from an expression of deep social and cultural divisions into an ordeal through which Edward Waverley must pass on his journey towards the exalted condition of landed proprietorship. Scott rehearses the English conquest of the Highlands and attempts at the same time to justify that action as an essential precondition for the greater progress of Scotland and the British nation. But he understands that in reenacting the 1745 rebellion, he is writing a story of the past in accordance with his own vision of history.

The modal mixture of Scott's fiction must be viewed against a tradition of fiction-writing that begins with the Gothic novelists of the late eighteenth and early nineteenth centuries. The first chapter of *Waverley* indicates that the Gothic retained a genuine vitality for Scott and for his reader:

Had I, for example, announced in my frontispiece, "Waverley, a Tale of Other Days," must not every novel reader have anticipated a castle scarce less than that of Udolpho, of which the eastern wing had long been uninhabited, and the keys either lost, or consigned to the care of some aged butler or housekeeper, whose trembling steps, about the middle of the second volume, were doomed to guide the hero, or heroine, to the ruinous precincts? Would not the owl have shrieked and the cricket cried in my very title-page? ... Again, had my title borne, "Waverley, a Romance from the German," what head so obtuse as not to image forth a profligate abbot, an oppressive duke, a secret and mysterious association of Rosycrucians and Illuminati, with all their properties of black cowls, caverns, daggers, electrical machines, trap-doors, and dark lanterns?[10]

As Jane Austen had done in *Northanger Abbey*, Scott defined his position as a novelist within and against the Gothic mode. His historical romances are not just one kind of challenge to Gothic conventions, but a dialectical response to Gothic romance. To grasp properly the place of Scott's fiction in literary history, we must see his novels as a countergenre to the Gothic, in which the forms of the Gothic are taken up and rendered as the conventions of an obsolescent literature, and at the same time preserved and modified. The forms of Gothic romance are represented in Scott's writing in order to be defamiliarized and then historicized. Scott expressed his conception of the uses of Gothic in his "Introduction" to Horace Walpole's *Castle of Otranto*. Scott sees Walpole's object in *Otranto* as one of presenting "such a picture of domestic life and manners, during the feudal times, as might actually have existed, and to paint it chequered and agitated by the action of supernatural machinery, such as the superstition of the period received as a matter of devout credulity ..."[11] As Scott sees it, Walpole's aim was to present a plausible and realistic picture of feudal society and to describe the consciousness of the times, "the superstition of the period" which believed in the force of the supernatural. For Walpole, Scott observes, the supernatural is a matter of machinery, a technique which represents accurately the feudal world-view, yet which appears to the modern reader precisely as a technique. Walpole wrote in *Otranto* a certain kind of "romantic narrative," one which, "though held impossible by more enlightened ages, was yet consonant with the faith of earlier times."[12]

While Scott's assessment of Walpole is a strong misreading rather than a piece of objective description, the "Introduction" tells us a great deal about Scott's own attitude towards the past, about his own sense of his motives for using what he calls "supernatural machinery."[13] The project described in the "Introduction" marks an essential difference between Scott's work and the classic Gothic novels. Scott's exploitation of the Gothic in *The Bride of Lammermoor* (1819) goes well beyond the use of supernatural elements to represent the feudal consciousness. Scott turns the Gothic mode against itself, using it to demystify the vision of the "superstitious eye," to draw a phrase from *The Bride of Lammermoor* (ch. 20; 289), and to reclaim the world for a certain kind of historical vision. Despite Scott's manifest interest in historical issues, the novel retains the key ideological prerogatives of Gothic fiction.[14] Scott openly disavows subjective epistemology and belief in the power of the supernatural, and offers detailed studies of social life against the gloomy fatalism of the novel's central action. But in its very setting, the Scotland of pre-Union days, more than 100 years before its date of composition, *The Bride* is ideologically motivated. The use of archaic character types displaces the threat to social order from its real contemporary locus in a growing mass of industrial laborers to a much older and less potent enemy, to an aristocratic figure from the distant past. Along with these

relatively simple strategies of historical distancing, the novel brings
to bear a Gothic background of omens and prophecies, legends of
usurpation and revenge, character types and stock symbols. By
association with the novel's feudal character, these anti-realistic
elements are ascribed to the archaic and obsolete consciousness of
the past.

Scott's strategies of association are typically a matter of tainting
his characters by contact with supernatural elements. Fergus MacIvor,
the cosmopolitan clan chief of *Waverley*, is profoundly affected by
the appearance of the Bodach Glas on the eve of what proves to be
his final battle. But while the Highlander is deeply moved, Scott allows
Waverley, and his reader, to remain at a distance from the supernatural version of events in which Fergus believes: "Edward had little
doubt that this phantom was the operation of an exhausted frame
and depressed spirits, working on the belief common to all
Highlanders in such superstitions" (*Waverley*, ch. 59; 269). As a
politician and military leader, Fergus stands as a recognizably modern
figure, an ambitious individual whose aims coincided closely with
those of the exiled regime. But his belief in the reality of the Bodach
Glas marks MacIvor as a clansman, a true Highlander beneath the
artificial surface of courtly manners and mores. In this brief scene,
Scott bestows the supernatural with a relative credence as an essential element of clan consciousness, of which a man born into the social
order of the clan would partake as a matter of course. But while
Fergus believes, Waverley, and the reader, are allowed to hesitate,
and thereby to assume a position of rational doubt.

This opposition between belief and disbelief, the shift between the
rational consciousness and the "superstitious eye," is a fundamental
element of Scott's fictional ideology. Scott's handling of the supernatural shows the kind of hesitation Tzvetan Todorov has defined
generically as the "uncanny":

In a world which is indeed our world, the one we know, a world without devils,
sylphides, or vampires, there occurs an event which cannot be explained by
the laws of this same familiar world. The person who experiences the event
must opt for one of two possible solutions. Either he is the victim of an illusion
of the senses, of a product of the imagination – and the laws of the world
then remain what they are; or else the event has indeed taken place, it is an
integral part of reality – but then this reality is controlled by laws unknown
to us.[15]

According to the generic laws proposed by Todorov, Edgar Ravenswood's uncertainty as to the reality of the spectre of Old Alice at the Mermaiden's well (*Bride*, ch. 23; 348–50) stands as an instance of the "fantastic": "Either the devil is an illusion, or he really exists, precisely like other living beings ... The fantastic occupies the duration of this uncertainty."[16] But in its "semantic" aspect, to borrow Todorov's category, the novel manifests the "uncanny." In an earlier encounter between Ravenswood and his lover (*Bride*, ch. 20; 289) the supernatural vision is clearly relegated to a subordinate position in the novel's hierarchy of perception, while the rational vision takes the high ground.

This shift between the "fantastic" and the "uncanny" is a recurrent movement of Scott's fiction. When Darsie Latimer of *Redgauntlet* (1824) discovers the tell-tale horseshoe sign on his forehead, he partakes, for a moment, of the archaic consciousness of which Hugh Redgauntlet is a prime exemplum. He shares, for an instant, in the sense of fatality which impels his uncle:

> Catching the reflection of my countenance in a large antique mirror which stood before me, I started again at the real or imaginary resemblance which my countenance, at that moment, bore to that of Herries. Surely my fate is somehow strangely interwoven with that of this mysterious individual.
>
> (*Redgauntlet*, ch. 7; 14)

Consistently projecting a position of relative credence, and with it the thematic corollary of the shift between belief in the supernatural and doubt of its force, the novel allows a double reading of its events. But the interpretative problem thus engendered is again resolved in the direction of the rational, of historical explanation. To the archaic vision of the feudal consciousness, the failure of Hugh Redgauntlet's revolt would appear as yet another repetition of the pattern of fatality which has gradually destroyed the family line. But to the nineteenth-century reader, gazing on the past from the temporal distance of some sixty years there is little mystery to the failure of the rebellion. Redgauntlet's scheme was bound to fail because of the moral weakness of the Stuart heir, the superior intelligence and military power of the Hanoverian army, and the ideological enervation of the Jacobite party. The hesitation between belief and disbelief registered in the novel allows the exploitation of the supernatural sense of fatality in the service of historical analysis.

Scott's disavowal of Gothic conventions in the opening chapter of *Waverley* is enacted repeatedly in his fiction. But realistic perception is reinforced in his novels by the very conventions he rejects as distortions of the real. In his mingling of history and fiction, realistic perception is defined and ratified by the vision of romance. Romance and realism are mutually constitutive, ways of seeing and writing the past defined by the specific context of their relationship within Scott's writing. Romance for Scott is a construction of the imagination. A source of delight and entertainment in moments of leisure, it is also a form of false consciousness, an untrue language, a source of distortion for which the rational vision must serve as the demystifying agent and the corrective. Yet romance is valuable to Scott for those very distortions of reality which are its failings. Scott sees romance as an evasion of the real, the language of irrationality, of illusion. Yet as a language of illusion, romance is a powerful instrument of historical revision. While Scott rejects the language of romance as a means of grasping the movements of history, he uses romance plots as a way of reshaping the past, of mastering history.

The motives of Scott's revisions can only be fully understood against the story of his life. The history Scott sought to master in his fiction is at once public and private. Scott wrote his own career over and over again in the careers of the Waverley heroes. In the process of transforming history, he revised the life of Scott, he altered his autobiography. This revision is not merely a matter of a few changes of names and places, but of a double transformation. The social experience of the author, which is already ideological, is itself transformed by Scott's fictional interpretation.

The modal tensions of the Waverley novels can be traced to Scott's conflicted sense of his own historical position.[17] Scott was a lawyer by training and occupation, a member of the professional middle class. He began his legal career as an advocate at the Scottish Court of Session, and in the course of his life held numerous legal and judicial positions. These included the office of Sheriff of Selkirkshire, a post which involved Scott in settling minor civil disturbances in a region dominated by large property-holders. Through his purchase of the land on which he built the Abbotsford estate, Scott became directly connected with the landowning class of the Border country. He made the original purchase of a small farm with money drawn from his earnings as an author and editor, and from his modest investment in John Ballantyne's publishing firm. Within a few months of the initial acquisition, Scott was planning to attach several adjacent farms to his property. A large portion of the profits later realized from his writing would be used to expand and improve the Abbotsford property. With the emoluments of his legal activities, his literary labors, and the investments that the popularity of his books made possible, Scott bought his way into the landed gentry. By gradually acquiring local properties as they came up for auction, he became, at least in his own ironic estimation, a "great laird."[18]

The Abbotsford estate is an architectural version of the political fantasy that animates the Waverley novels, the dream of landed establishment.[19] Abbotsford expresses two conflicting motives: the desire for upward mobility, the parvenu's dream of making it rich and buying a country estate; and a longing for the restoration of the ancient landed establishment, and with it, the social relations of an older and better world. These opposing drives are visible in another autobiographical text, in Scott's affair with Williamina Belsches. In his extended account of the affair, Edgar Johnson has observed the significant social distance beween the young barrister and the daughter of Sir John Belsches. As Johnson succinctly puts it: "The daughter of a baronet and the granddaughter of an earl enjoyed far loftier rank than the son of a cadet branch of a numerous clan, whose father was a mere writer to the Signet."[20] Since the story of the relationship is widely known, a brief sketch will do service here. Scott had known Williamina Belsches since his early youth and, over a period of several years, had fallen in love with her, finally proposing to her in his early twenties. Her responses to Scott's repeated advances were always ambiguous, but Scott persuaded himself that Miss Belsches was pledged to him, even as she was falling in love with a man who was more her social equal than was Scott. When her engagement was announced, Scott was shocked and angry, and his journal shows that a deep sense of injury remained with him until the end of his life.[21] While critics have drawn the obvious parallels between the Belsches affair and the events and characters of the novels, especially *The Bride*, the sexual element of the affair and its relationship to the social has generally been neglected.[22] Reenacted in *The Bride*, in the affair of Edgar Ravenswood and Lucy Ashton, the relationship takes on a powerful element of sado-masochism, with Ravenswood attacking his lover and himself in a single, grand gesture of revenge.

The larger structural ambiguity of Scott's social position is visible both in the characterological organization of the novels and in the mixed sympathies of the so-called "heroes." In *Waverley*, the components of the Jacobite movement are divided among several characters. Flora MacIvor embodies the idealistic element of Jacobitism, while her brother represents its opportunism. Evan Dhu represents the crude, but genuine, nobility of the Highland character in offering to exchange his life for his chief's, while Callum Beg, sniping at anyone he imagines to be an enemy of the clan, represents the other, the darker, side of the clansman. When Scott wants us to see the spiritual side of Jacobitism or the traditional virtues of the Highland social order, he brings in Flora or Evan Dhu, and when he wants to remind us of the ambition or the destructive parochialism of the movement, he brings in Fergus or Callum Beg.

The intentional structure of the novel can be broken down into an ideological deep structure, a structure in which the light and dark heroes and heroines, the good and the bad Highlanders, can be regarded as the poles of a semantic opposition which finds a resolution of sorts in the mixed figure of Edward Waverley. Waverley's marriage to the light heroine, the domesticated daughter of the Jacobite Baron of Bradwardine, is a way of resolving the destructive antagonism of the present order with the past. But what the marriage of Waverley and Rose achieves is not a true synthesis. The problem of how to reconcile past and present is resolved by the simple destruction of one of the novel's essential elements, the dark side of Jacobitism.

Scott acts as a sort of peacemaker in *Waverley*, self-consciously reenacting the struggles of the past in order to preserve the traditional virtues amid the rapid progress of the present. But the imaginative project of preserving the ways and manners of past societies that Scott describes in the "Postscript" to *Waverley* is not a dialectical process of cancelling and preserving, but the far less complicated one of eliminating that part of a duality which poses a threat to the idea of a stable present. *Waverley* begins with good Jacobites and bad ones, and ends with the major figures of the rebellion either dead or domesticated. The novel resolves its basic semantic opposition by taming or simply killing off the figures who represent the darker side of the old order. Having projected the older forms of social life as other, as obsolete and dangerous despite their virtues, the novel then rescues the virtuous representatives of the past and destroys those it has conceived as dangerous.

With their consistently mixed loyalties, Scott's protagonists are not simply reflections of his own mixed class affiliations, but elements of his artistic strategies for resolving the oppositions engendered, in part, by his social position. In the figures of Waverley and Ravenswood, Scott projects a solution to the problem, at once artistic and political, which he has posed for himself: the problem of reconciling the progress of the present moment with the ways of feudal and pre-feudal societies. Yet while Scott appears in *Waverley* to have balanced the loss of the past with the progress of the present,[23] there is a contradiction in Edward Waverley's ascent into landed property. Waverley's relative passivity would seem to make him a proper figure to inherit property, according to Alexander Welsh's formula, suitable material for the landed aristocracy whose restoration Scott fantasized in the form of his Abbotsford.[24] But Abbotsford, as we know, was not inherited by Scott. While Waverley will inherit his uncle's property, he collaborates with Colonel Talbot to purchase Tully-Veolan. The restoration of the Baron of Bradwardine to his estate is thus accomplished through a gesture which runs counter to Scott's own Burkean notion of landed property as a power to be transmitted by inheritance from generation to generation.[25] A limited reconciliation of the old order with the new is achieved in *Waverley*, but only through a prior act of appropriation. In *The Bride of Lammermoor*, Scott once again locates his central thematic opposition in the figure of a hero-like character. Edgar Ravenswood combines the residual loyalty of a feudal aristocrat to the memory of his family's ascendancy with the rational and moderate disposition of his family's bourgeois nemesis. The fascinating twist of *The Bride* is that Scott provides the possibility of resolving the novel's central social conflict through the affair of Ravenswood and Lucy Ashton, but then describes the historical and psychological processes by which the projected marriage is thwarted.

Despite these unresolved tensions, Scott's insertion of a relatively passive character has an important unifying effect, giving the reader a dual perspective on the events of the novels. The figure who appears to be on both sides at once permits what seems to be a balanced view of the past, serving as a guide to the ways of the past, of the men and women who peopled the pre-history of bourgeois society. Edward

Waverley's journey serves at once to bring Scott's hero to a recognition of the "real history" of his life and to redefine the relationship between a fictional England and its northern counterpart. With his journey complete, a mature and knowing Waverley can regard the defeat of the Jacobite rebels as an unfortunate, but necessary, event in the reestablishment of a peaceful and harmonious British kingdom.

The "Postscript" to *Waverley* reinforces this conception of historical change. The tone of reportorial ease registers a sense of satisfaction, not to say complacency, with things as they are:

There is no European nation which, within the course of half a century, has undergone so complete a change as this kingdom of Scotland. The effects of the insurrection of 1745 − the destruction of the patriarchal power of the Highland chiefs − the abolition of the heritable jurisdictions of the Lowland nobility and the barons − the total eradication of the Jacobite party, which, averse to intermingle with the English, or adopt their customs, long continued to pride themselves upon maintaining ancient Scottish manners and customs, − commenced this innovation. The gradual influx of wealth, and extension of commerce, have since united to render the present people of Scotland a class of beings as different from their grandfathers as the existing English are from those of Queen Elizabeth's time … But the change, though steadily and rapidly progressive, has, nevertheless, been gradual; and like those who drift down the stream of a deep and smooth river, we are not aware of the progress we have made, until we fix our eye on the now distant point from which we have drifted. Such of the present generation as can recollect the last twenty or twenty-five years of the eighteenth century, will be fully aware of the truth of this statement …

Numerous passages could be cited from the novels to demonstrate Scott's preference for the ways of the past. But what we find in the "Postscript" is a calm acceptance of the changes which have occurred in the period of "sixty years since." The "total eradication of the Jacobite party" recorded by Scott's observer has had the beneficial effect of eliminating "much absurd political prejudice" and the detrimental one of destroying some of the finer virtues of old Scotland. Scott's equivocation here is masterful. His profession of sympathy for "folks of the old leaven" (*Waverley*, ch. 72; 400−01) is balanced by a sense that their political biasses were, after all, better lost than preserved. As Scott very well knew, without its "political prejudices," the "Jacobite party" would have been no Jacobite party at all.

What we find in the "Postscript," along with Scott's own quietly expressed political prejudices, is the sense of a comfortable distance between past and present. This fictively established temporal distance creates a feeling of ease for the reader about his relationship with the past, reassuring him of the legitimacy of his own historical position and the impartiality of his perspective on the past. Scott comments on the force of his revisionary strategies in the final chapter of *Old Mortality*, in a dialogue between his narrator, Peter Pattieson, and a feminine reader. Pattieson begins the chapter, entitled "Conclusion," by declaring his aversion to writing a conclusion: "I had determined to waive the task of a concluding chapter, leaving to the reader's imagination the arrangements which must necessarily take place after Lord Evandale's death" (*Old Mortality*, "Conclusion;" 340). The "Conclusion" is a way of satisfying the reader's demand for a felicitous ending and tweaking her nose at the same time, at once fulfilling and mocking the expectation of a happy unity, and reminding the reader of the novel's fictive status. The point of the dialogue between Pattieson and Miss Martha Buskbody would seem to be that the novel, while it will undoubtedly be read and judged by the likes of Miss Buskbody, was not written for the obtuse reader who relishes the forms of sentimental romance.

But the question the "Conclusion" raises (without answering) is that of just what kind of reader the novel was written for. Miss Buskbody is finally a parody not only of the romantic reader, but of Scott's own effort to compose a fiction of restoration. Scott accuses his "feminine reader" of shallowness in her interpretation of the narrative. What she wants is not the story Pattieson has written, but one which will satisfy her debased aesthetic appetites, which will give her "glimpses of sunshine" and signs of "future felicity." Scott calls attention here to his contradictory treatment of the fairy-tale patterns of romance. In her demand for a happy resolution, Miss Buskbody has missed the true significance of Pattieson's historical narrative. But the comical exchange between Pattieson and Miss Buskbody cannot be understood as a realistic attack on the false values of romance, nor as the product of an anachronistic partiality for indeterminacy. The "Conclusion" is an expression of Scott's recognition of the inevitable failure of fiction as an instrument for containing the destructive forces of the past. Scott cannot be identified with either one of his framing figures here more than the other.

To place the author on the side of a truthful Pattieson against a superficial Miss Buskbody is to ignore a fundamental tension in Scott's attitude toward his art. Scott knows that he has failed to find in his elaborate legerdemain a satisfactory resolution to the conflicts he has staged in his narrative. While he has sought, like Peter Pattieson, to present an "unbiassed" account of the past, he is acutely conscious of the limits of his own fictions. He understands that like Miss Buskbody raised to a higher power, he has interpreted the past in accordance with literary convention, rather than simply recording it as it happened. In the "Conclusion," he acknowledges these limits, yet simultaneously asserts the power of his fictions to resist the effects of historical change.

Scott's historiography is an untidy amalgam of conflicting notions about the relationship between fiction and historical reality and about the power of the imagination to reshape the course of history by means of story. This is not to suggest that Scott was a metahistorian in the ironic mode of Hayden White, but simply to allow for the complexities of his art. Writing of Scott's ambivalence toward the imagination on the one hand and history on the other, Frederick Pottle has argued that Scott "does not, like the more advanced Romantics, believe in the creative imagination as revelatory of truth." With his perception "rooted firmly in the eighteenth century,"[26] Scott regarded fiction as, at best, a form of sophisticated amusement. Pottle does not claim, however, that Scott was merely a romancer, whose sole intention was to entertain. Observing in Scott a fascination with the facts of the past, Pottle sees at the foundation of his artistic activity "a clear, sharp, undistorted, 'realistic' perception of things," along with a "determination to keep it clear from the play of the imagination."[27] Some of Scott's own remarks on the relationship between fiction and history suggest that he did, indeed, regard his novels as works of imagination, products of fancy inferior to histories in purpose and effect:

I aver, on the contrary, that by introducing the busy and the youthful to "truths severe in fairy fiction," I am doing a real service to the more ingenious among them; for the love of knowledge wants but a beginning — the least spark will give fire when the train is properly prepared; and having been interested in fictitious adventures, ascribed to an historical period and characters, the reader begins next to be anxious to learn what the facts really were, and how far the novelist has justly represented them. But even where the mind of the more careless reader remains satisfied with the light perusal he has afforded to a tale of fiction, he will still lay down the book with a degree of knowledge, not perhaps of the most accurate kind, but such as he might not otherwise have acquired.

("Prefatory Letter" to *Peveril of the Peak*, lxx–lxxi)

Speaking here as the anonymous "Author of Waverley," Scott justifies the writing of historical romances as a means of leading his readers to the inherently more serious study of history. His service to the "busy and youthful" is to incite a desire to know history, to discover "what the facts really were." With this knowledge in hand, the curious reader can determine the degree of the novelist's fidelity to the facts.

Removed as it is from the context of Scott's fictional "Prefatory Letter" to *Peveril*, the passage seems to reflect Scott's belief in an essential difference between fiction and historical fact. Novels are mere fictions, fabrications which can evoke the reader's curiosity about the past, but which cannot give the truth of the past. History, by implication, is a body of facts about the past, about things as they actually happened. We might infer from this that Scott, assuming the greater seriousness of history, was willing to make only a few modest claims for his fictions. But the "Author of Waverley" is not simply Scott's mouthpiece here. The entertainer who dresses the past in "fairy fiction" with the hope that his humble tales might help lead his readers toward true knowledge is yet another of Scott's fictive personae, on a par with Jedidiah Cleisbotham or Peter Pattieson. In Scott's "Prefatory Letter" to *Peveril*, the "Author of Waverley" is simply one voice in a dialogue about the nature and purpose of historical romance, representing a position that Scott adopted and abandoned according to the exigencies of composition.

That Scott was, at least in part, a product of the eighteenth century is undeniable. But to suggest that he is a romancer here and a realist there is to oversimplify. Scott's attitude toward the imagination was far more complicated than Pottle's formulation, for all its salutary clarity, would allow. Scott clearly did not believe in the capacity of the imagination to reveal the truth of things as they were. But as we read his introductory chapters, and as we reread his narratives against the context of his own comments on his writing, it becomes equally clear that Scott believed in the power of the imagination to revise the patterns of history.

Scott challenges the validity of literary forms for representing the

the past by appealing to a reality beyond the boundaries of fiction. But he undermines his own essays in accurate historical representation by submitting the past and its textual records to the transforming power of romance. Despite Scott's studied manipulations, the novels are marked by a disjunction between imaginative play and realistic perception. Scott knew that his novels were not copies of historical reality, but stories about an imagined past. Yet at certain moments he wrote as if he believed he were telling the truth about things as they were, as if he had somehow forgotten the gap between imagination and reality. There is, particularly in the earlier fiction, a tension between Scott as historical romancer, the trickster who writes history as he wishes it had happened, attempting to fool the credulous reader with his clever illusions of the past, and Scott the realist, writing a straight narrative of the past, faithfully depicting things as they were. While Scott knew that he was concocting stories about history, he still held to a notion of historical truth and intelligibility. He regarded his fabrications as imaginative works written, at least in some part, in the service of historical veracity. His seemingly casual treatment of his own fictions and his skepticism about the power of language to grasp historical reality coexist with a belief that there was a truth to be told about the past, that the past was objectively there, and that it could be accurately understood and presented from the perspective of the present. Along with the author who writes extended reflections on his own historiographical methods, we find a Scott who wants to write real history, to give his reader the unvarnished truth of the past. This contradiction, with its formal corollary in the jarring admixture of romance and realism which runs throughout the novels, remains unresolved, even in the most self-conscious of his works.

Scott observes, on the one hand, that his fictions are not to be confused with history. There is fiction and there is history, and while the truths of history may be decked out in fictions, the two worlds cannot intersect. Yet the two modes are so closely intertwined in Scott's writing that one is often indistinguishable from the other. The boundary between fiction and fact, romance and reality, is crossed and recrossed repeatedly in the novels without much visible concern for philosophical or generic consistency. If history subverts romance, then romance, in turn, alters history, not merely softening and blurring its harsh outlines, changing its colors slightly, but actually reinventing the past, making a new story out of history.

2

THE REEMPLOTMENT OF
REBELLION: *WAVERLEY* AND
OLD MORTALITY

Near the end of *Waverley*, Scott's hero feels himself "entitled to say firmly, though perhaps with a sigh, that the romance of his life was ended, and that its real history had now commenced" (ch. 60; 281). But at this moment Scott's historical romance is far from over. The passage marks not the end of romance in the novel, but the end of Waverley's romantic phase.[1] Romance is apparently reduced here to the status of mere fictional mode, to an artificial and therefore false way of perceiving things. "Real history" will be what Waverley experiences henceforth. If we read the novel as the story of the hero's education, as an account of his growth from ignorance to wisdom, we might regard the passage as meaning that Waverley has finally shed his romantic delusions and arrived at a true perception of reality, and as implying that Scott himself is on the side of "real history" and against "romance."[2] But we cannot simply identify Scott's perspective with that of his character. To regard the anti-romantic temper of Waverley's perceptions here as an expression of the author's position is to neglect the context for the passage which Scott provides in his reflections on the power of art. The "real history" of Waverley's life has for Scott the same fictive status as its "romance." The difference between author and character rests in Scott's awareness that much as he might try to represent the past in his language, he is limited to telling stories about it, and his knowledge that the "romance" which Waverley declares to have ended on his stay in Northumberland has some consolations to offer for the consequences of "real history." Scott knows that, like his hero, he can know history only by way of his fictions.

Waverley's moment of insight at Fasthwaite brings to an end a long episode in his convention-bound life. If Waverley now begins to perceive his life through the perceptual grid of "real history," Scott persists in his fictionalizing of history. Romance, as Scott conceives it in *Waverley*, cannot provide a true description of reality. But it can still serve Scott's version of British history, it can still be used to ratify Scott's own vision of the past. Romance is an eminently useful literary convention for Scott. If it is a form of delusion, then it is a delusion which he uses to great advantage. While he suggests that romance is a form of false consciousness, Scott employs it as a way of excluding history from his fiction, of keeping the past at a distance and thereby reducing its disruptive force.

We are repeatedly reminded in the novel of Scott's self-conscious fabrication and of the deformative effect of historical representation on historical reality.[3] In the final chapter of the narrative, we find ourselves gazing at a picture of Waverley and Fergus MacIvor, a picture which is quite clearly a misrepresentation of the events and relationships depicted in the novel. In the dinner-parlour of Tully-Veolan, the Baron of Bradwardine, having returned now to a restored version of his patrimonial estate, finds an "addition" to "the old arrangement": "... a large and spirited painting, representing Fergus MacIvor and Waverley in their Highland dress; the scene a wild, rocky, and mountainous pass, down which the clan were descending in the background." The painting, we are told, was "taken from a spirited sketch, drawn while they were in Edinburgh by a young man of high genius, and had been painted on a full-length scale by an eminent London artist." What we see through the eyes of the Baron is the past at a double-remove, a painting rendered by an artist in London from a sketch drawn by an artist in Edinburgh. The painting is a picture of a picture, a production of an earlier production which can only allow the viewer a mediated perception of the past. Yet it is "beheld with admiration and deeper feelings," and it even draws "tears to the Baron's eyes" (ch. 71; 396–97).

This metafictional moment in the dinner-parlour must be seen as an element in the strategy of domestication practiced by Scott throughout the novel, most fully in the concluding chapters.[4] Scott openly thematizes the domesticating force of his writing in *Waverley*. He rehearses the English conquest of the Highlands and attempts at the same time to justify that action as an essential precondition for the greater progress of Scotland and the British nation. Yet he understands that in reproducing the historical events of the 1745 rebellion, he is telling a story about history which is invested with his own political biasses. Scott allows his reader to shed a few tears along with the Baron. But he quietly notes that the picture which draws tears to the Baron's eye is a second-hand rendering, in which the real thing has been drawn and then painted over. In this picture of a sketch, the many pictures drawn in *Waverley* are collapsed into one, and thereby distorted, drawn or written over. Scott knows that in appealing to the sentiments of his reader, he is revising his own stories of the past. In bringing the opposing sides in the novel's central political conflict back together, he is performing a similar gesture. By perpetuating the Waverley line through a male heir and restoring the Bradwardine estate to a semblance of its former grandeur, Scott produces his own comforting illusions. His intention is that just as the arrangement of the painting and the armour on the wall of the dinner-parlour elicits "admiration and deeper feelings" from the wedding guests, so will his arrangement of scenes evoke a satisfied response from the reader.

In *Waverley*, the preferred method of dealing with disruptive political desire is to frame it within the boundaries of a sentimental portrait. Scott's art quells rebellion and puts to death the principal agents of the revolt, reviving its victims only to remove from them the taint of subversion. Fergus MacIvor, the most determined and dangerous of the Highland Jacobites, is rendered harmless in the dinner-parlour portrait, depicted as a friend of Edward Waverley, a comrade-in-arms, a fellow wearer of the tartan. The painting memorializes Fergus for his friends and comrades. But the memorial is only necessary and possible because Fergus, and the social order which he represented, are now dead. The very conditions which have elevated Waverley to the position of a great landholder and which have allowed him and Talbot to restore Tully-Veolan have destroyed Fergus and eradicated the limited political influence of the clans.[5]

The reader who allows himself to be taken in by Scott's pictorial trickery will, for the moment, forget the historical circumstances of Fergus's demise. Scott's art serves to soften the harsher scenes of economic and social reality, creating at once an illusion of presence and a sense of distance between past and present. The painting in the dinner-parlour is compared favorably to one by Raeburn, "whose

Highland chiefs do all but walk out of the canvas" (ch. 71; 397), for its likeness to life. What the painting accomplishes, however, is not a faithful rendering of its subjects, but a freezing of narrative time, a reduction of the events leading up to and following the rebellion into a still picture. The portrait transforms history into a moment of soldierly affection, in which no one is killed and no one's tartans get dirty.

Beyond the limits of Scott's political ken is the larger context of British colonialism in the eighteenth and nineteenth centuries. *Waverley* is an imaginary representation of a prior ideological subtext, of the unfortunate, but necessary, defeat and subjugation of an older and less civilized society. Of course, Scott did not imagine himself as an apologist for British imperialism. Yet in *Waverley* he serves as a sort of jovial ideologue of progress, deliberately and skillfully altering the historical events which are his ostensible subject. The political fantasies elaborated in Scott's representations of the past have both a positive and a negative, a productive and an ideological function. Scott's pictures of the past serve at once to defer the effects of history, to suppress the force of the real and to perpetuate the patterns of domination the novel disguises.[6] In recapitulating the old story of conquest and stabilization, Scott creates another Scotland, a picture of the people who inhabited the country in the mid-eighteenth century, of their social world, and of their consciousness. The Scotland of *Waverley*, as Scott was aware, is fictively produced. But it is produced — and here we must draw the line between ourselves and the author — in such a way as to ratify the status quo. It is Scott's knowledge of the national past, a knowledge which is far from disinterested, which prescribes the boundaries of the world we discover in the scenes of *Waverley*.

The lengthy discursive footnotes which appear in the Waverley novels might seem to indicate a deep anxiety on Scott's part about the perceived historicity of his work. But behind the scholarly demeanor projected in the notes is an author who is playing with stories of the past, historical records, anecdotes and legends, who is blending these disparate materials to make historical romances. With some important qualifications, the dualistic version of Scott first promoted by David Daiches can thus be retained.[7] Scott was ambivalent not only in his attitude towards progress, but in his attitude towards fiction as a means of grasping history, and in his conception of his own authorial powers as a writer of historical fiction.

As he approaches Tully-Veolan for the first time, Waverley's observations fluctuate between a harshly detailed rendering of life in the hamlet and a "picturesque" rendering of the same object:

The houses seemed miserable in the extreme, especially to an eye accustomed to the smiling neatness of English cottages. They stood, without any respect for regularity, on each side of a straggling kind of unpaved street, where children, almost in a primitive state of nakedness, lay sprawling, as if to be crushed by the hoofs of the first passing horse.

As he moves through the hamlet, Waverley finds "more pleasing objects": "Three or four village girls, returning from the well or brook with pitchers and pails upon their heads ... [who] with their thin shortgowns and single petticoats, bare arms, legs, and feet, uncovered heads and braided hair, somewhat resembled Italian forms of landscape." Here Waverley performs a typical gesture of imaginative transformation. His perceptions of the Scottish landscape early in the novel are "picturesque" in their operation, and in such moments as these, Scott's own fondness for that popular idiom is registered:[8] "Nor could a lover of the picturesque have challenged either the elegance of their costume, or the symmetry of their shape" (ch. 8; 72).

But the description of Waverley's observations on passing through the hamlet establishes a distance between Scott's narrative voice and the perceptions of his character. The picturesque vision which finds "elegance of costume" and "symmetry of shape" in the indigent inhabitants of the decaying hamlet is countered by a perspective peculiarly "English,"

although, to say the truth, a mere Englishman in search of the *comfortable*, a word peculiar to his native tongue, might have wished the clothes less scanty, the feet and legs somewhat protected from the weather, the head and complexion shrouded from the sun, or perhaps might have thought the whole person and dress considerably improved by a plentiful application of spring water, with a *quantum sufficit* of soap.   (ch. 8; 72–73)

By suggesting the need for better clothing and a good bath, Scott challenges the picturesque perspective as a distortion of the simple facts of existence. Beyond what a "mere Englishman" would see in the hamlet of Tully-Veolan is the depressing economic condition of the place. Writing as if he were an agricultural reformer studying the social life of the Lowlands, Scott notes such details as the arrangement of cottages in the village, the distances between buildings, and the kinds of crops raised in the small and ragged enclosures. The prospect which Waverley views on his arrival is clearly in need of improvement:

> The broken ground on which the village was built had never been levelled; so that the inclosures presented declivities of every degree, here rising like terraces, there sinking like tanpits. The dry-stone walls which fenced, or seemed to fence, (for they were sorely breached) these hanging gardens of Tully-Veolan, were intersected by a narrow lane leading to the common field, where the joint labour of the villagers cultivated alternate ridges and patches of rye, oats, barley, and pease, each of such minute extent, that at a little distance, the unprofitable variety of the surface resembled a tailor's book of patterns. (ch. 8; 74)

Scott details here the material causes of the "depressing" prospect which he has described in the village. Against the "picturesque" version of things, he gives an explanation which is economic in its bases. This is the voice of the "philosophical" historian, making connections between the primitive social life and the outmoded economic system of the village. The effect is to destroy the "picturesque" prospect discovered by Waverley, to debunk the hero's vision with a "realistic" account of the forces which have brought poverty to the village.

Near the dunghill and stack of turf which fence in the cottages of the hamlet is the park of Tully-Veolan estate, its arches appearing as "masses of mutilated stone" which, according to local tradition, were once "rampant bears," the heraldic symbols of the Bradwardine family. By connecting the two prospects in Waverley's perspective, Scott asserts a linkage between the depressed hamlet, with its outmoded runrig system of cultivation, its impoverished and poorly dressed inhabitants and its atmosphere of decrepitude, and the decaying symbols of ancient feudal power. This is the Scott so much admired by Lukács, the great realist who describes with seemingly remarkable accuracy and insight the social and economic conditions which give shape to the larger historical conflicts depicted in the Waverley novels. But the sombre historical vision which yields this bleak picture of the hamlet alternates with an effort to evade the dismal prospect of rural poverty. Andrew Hook gets at the motive of these shifts of perspective in his observation that "Scott seems to struggle to find something picturesque about the scene."[9] Scott sets two conflicting ways of seeing beside one another, using the realistic to debunk the picturesque, and the picturesque to escape the grim vision of his own realism. The picturesque is destroyed by the realistic, but is quickly reconstituted as a kind of palliative for Waverley and for the reader.

In the early chapters of the novel, Scott serves as a sort of tour-guide, leading Waverley and the reader to the various attractions of his native country. But Scott is a tour-guide with a conscience, who cannot help steering his visitors through a decaying Lowland village on the way to an ancient feudal estate. Touring is not a politically innocent activity in *Waverley*; nor is the picturesque vision which Waverley brings to his tour of Scotland merely the naive aesthetic predisposition of an inexperienced young man. The avenue leading to the Baron's house represents to Waverley a moment of repose. As he gazes down the avenue toward the manor-house, he remarks to himself that the "effect[s]" of the scene were "those which a painter loves to represent ..." The appeal of the scene for Waverley is its capacity for exciting "ideas of rest and seclusion," "solitude and repose," for shifting his imagination away from the "misery and dirt" (ch. 8; 76) of the village and producing in his mind a sense that he is in another world, sheltered from the harsh effects of the village scene.

Waverley's experience of Scotland in these early chapters is predominantly pictorial. He is a tourist, an English soldier on leave from his regiment, and his perceptions of Scotland are initially those of a well-disposed stranger curious to observe close-up the many points of interest of a new country. But tourism in *Waverley* also involves a gesture of appropriation, the assimilation of the Scottish landscape by the visiting Englishman. Edward Waverley is hardly a passive observer of Scottish scenes. He is continually making a work of art out of the landscape. Waverley brings to the landscape a taste for the picturesque and the romantic which leads him to transform reality into pictures, to render the world into an occasion for aesthetic experience, as a scene in a painting or a work of literature. The avenue leading to the manor-house becomes a picture which allows the traveler to efface from his mind the sordid details of the village scene. The definitive gesture for Waverley is one of aestheticizing the world outside of his imagination, of making pictures as a way of evading reality.

Waverley's arrival at the Baron's estate is an occasion for Scott to remind us of the effects of the hero's early reading. Scott has already told us that as a result of "a desultory habit of reading" (ch. 3; 31), the young man is excessively fond of romances. Waverley's activities as a tourist are linked with his tendencies to daydreaming and with his fanciful excursions into the realm of romance. At Waverley-Honour, he had devoured romantic literature along with his aunt and uncle's stories of the family past, indulging in his own imaginative recreations of that past in a corner of the library. At Tully-Veolan, the romances in which Waverley had reveled in his uncle's library seem to him to have become a living reality. Chastened by the "dirt and misery" of Tully-Veolan village, Waverley's imagination is revivified in the atmosphere of the manor-house. He first sees the house without its residents, and "the whole scene still maintained the monastic illusion which the fancy of Waverley had conjured up" (ch. 8; 78). The implication of the passage is that Waverley's fancy, shaped by his limited literary and social experience at Waverley-Honour, requires the kind of scene available at Tully-Veolan on which to work its transformations. Tully-Veolan serves as a sort of prop to Waverley's fancy, as a material stimulus for the production of romantic situations.

Scott's purpose goes beyond the relatively simple one of illustrating the effects of Waverley's early education in fanciful literature. His aim is not merely to demonstrate Waverley's ignorance and naiveté, but to render the fictionalizing of reality, a process that yields an image far more appealing to a mind of romantic cast than the original materials would allow. What we see here is a romantic imagination acting out its wishes through the medium of the Scottish landscape. When Waverley tells himself that he is "actually in the land of military and romantic adventures," he is, in one sense, quite right. But he is there primarily by means of his own imaginative activity, rather than because of any objective properties of his environment. Waverley remakes his environment in accordance with the conventions of the picturesque and the romantic. He finds in the landscape the images which he wishes to find, which he himself has placed there.

Waverley's visit with the Baron gives him plenty of prime material with which to feed his active fancy, including frequent glimpses of Scottish manners and customs. The Baron throws a banquet on the occasion of Waverley's arrival, presiding over it in the ritual manner of the Bradwardine family. After a night of heavy drinking at the

Baron's table, Waverley falls into a quarrel with a neighboring laird, which is settled by Waverley's host, in accordance with tradition. He goes on hunting parties, converses with his host's charming daughter, and views scenery rich with the history of ancient Scottish families. On a fox-hunt, Waverley and the Baron exchange their views on history, and their dialogue reflects the processes of Waverley's imagination. The Baron recollects the "cold, dry, hard outlines which history delineates." Against the Baron's stiff-necked empiricism, Waverley brings his enlivening fancy. He "loved to fill up and round the sketch with the colouring of a warm and vivid imagination, which gives light and life to the actors and speakers in the drama of past ages." The Baron's "minute narratives" become "fresh subjects" for Waverley, "a new mine of incident and character" for the exercise of the young man's vigorous imagination (ch. 13; 124).

The news of the creagh is yet another source of excitement for Waverley, an incident that further stimulates his curiosity about the Highlands. Rose expresses her fear that the incident will lead to a feud with the Highlanders, and recalls a bloody skirmish which occurred some years before in which several Highlanders were killed. But Waverley is less interested at this moment in the safety of Tully-Veolan and its residents than in the possibility of high adventure. What matters to him is not the threat of violence posed to the unarmed inhabitants of the estate, but the fact that Rose has such marvelous stories to relate:

Here was a girl scarce seventeen, the gentlest of her sex, both in temper and appearance, who had witnessed with her own eyes such a scene as he had used to conjure up in his imagination, as only occurring in ancient times, and spoke of it coolly, as one very likely to recur. He felt at once the impulse of curiosity, and that slight sense of danger which only serves to heighten its interest.
(ch. 15; 153)

Waverley thus perceives events which not only have a disturbing political significance, but which pose a threat to the welfare of his hosts as actualizations of his own imaginings. Neglecting the tensions between the Lowland aristocracy and the Highland clans reflected in the creagh and the danger which a protracted quarrel might pose to an estate disarmed by government order, Waverley regards the theft as if it were merely a taunting aftertaste of the scene which Rose had witnessed when the clansmen had attacked the house itself.

In the old Gothic library of Waverley-Honour, Waverley had exercised his imagination on the relatively mundane materials of his family's history, transforming the rambling narratives of his aging relatives through "that internal sorcery by which past or imaginary events are presented in action, as it were, to the eye of the muser" (ch. 4; 40). At Tully-Veolan, Waverley's imagination works not merely on "storied monuments" and fragments of family and local lore, but on actual events. Here, Waverley considers himself to be in a world commensurate with his romantic imagination, where he need no longer conjure over old stories, but may witness first-hand, and perhaps even take part in, the great adventures of which he has hitherto merely dreamed.

It is, of course, Waverley's narrow education in romance which makes the life of the Baron and the Highland chieftain immensely attractive to him. Absorbed in the plots and images of the romances which are the main stock of his uncle's library, Waverley grows up in an atmosphere of unreality. At Waverley-Honour, the life of literature takes predominance over the actualities of the present. In the seclusion of their northern estate, Rachel and Sir Everard have fallen out of touch with the realities of English politics. Their own sympathies are grounded in a nostalgia for the dashing figures of family history, for the heroes of an idealized past, rather than in a genuine commitment to the dynastic claims of the Stuarts. Untempered by the harsh facts of the present, their political attitudes are as much a product of fancy as the stories which the youthful Edward concocts from family legends. Their political activities consist mainly of recounting the exploits of Nigel Waverley, a devoted servant of Queen Mary, who arrived at the door of Waverley-Honour bleeding from a mortal wound received in battle with the forces of the Protestant usurper.

Waverley-Honour is an enclave of dreamers, a haven from history. Its residents interpret the world outside through the obscuring layer of a heroic past, through a screen of legend which conceals the conditions of the present. Sir Everard is not a contemporary Nigel, but rather a sort of armchair Jacobite. His politics are merely a family legacy, an outmoded prejudice which he and his sister Rachel nurse in their old age. His celibate bachelorhood is the sexual corollary of his Jacobitism. When Everard's courtship of a young woman proved unsuccessful, he gave up on real romance and retired into a quiet bachelorhood on his estate. He remains celibate, avoiding any further forays into the perilous world of courtship and marriage. Edward is the heir-apparent of Everard's political prejudices as well as of his estate. But Edward's Jacobitism is more clearly a mixture of politics and sex. Edward engages in a fruitless courtship with Flora MacIvor, who is herself, not accidentally, I think, celibate. While Waverley persists in his courting of Flora, he remains attached to the Jacobite cause. His growing attraction to Rose Bradwardine parallels his disenchantment with Flora and Fergus and the cause for which they stand, his friendship with Colonel Talbot, and the movement toward a realistic perception of his experience.

Scott is not widely admired for his depictions of the relations between the sexes. In *Waverley*, the feelings usually associated with intense erotic attachment are manifested in deep ideological commitments. Flora is a "celibate for political ends,"[10] whose only real passion is for the exiled Stuart monarch and those who sacrifice themselves for his cause. Fergus suggests, with only partial humor, that Flora's heart belongs to a hero of the Stuart cause from ages past, one Captain Wogan, who lost his life doing battle for the true king. "Loyalty," says Fergus, is Flora's "ruling passion." "Since she could spell an English book," he tells Waverley,

She has been in love with the memory of the gallant Captain Wogan, who renounced the service of the usurper Cromwell to join the standard of Charles II, marched a handful of cavalry from London to the Highlands to join Middleton, then in arms for the king, and at length died gloriously in the royal cause.   (ch. 27; 275)

This mingling of love with royalist politics is reflected in the elegiac verse Flora composed for the Captain, and which Fergus sends to Waverley as a ploy to encourage the well-connected young Englishman in his suit for Flora's hand. As long as Waverley's attachment to Flora persists, he partakes of this blended desire.

Waverley's Jacobitism is a politics of unrequited love. Like his passion for Flora, his royalist sentiments persist precisely because they are merely dreams. The figure Waverley longs for is a product of his own fancy, shaped by his education in romance. The Flora he desires is a literary type, such as Waverley would have encountered in his solitary reading, which becomes a prop for his overly active imagination. Flora's resistance to Waverley's advances only increases his passion. The less accessible she is, the more distant she is from him, the greater is his desire.

Waverley's recognition that "the romance of his life was ended" and its "real history" has begun is at once an aesthetic and political turning point, for both character and novel. Romance is the genre of fantasy in *Waverley*, political and sexual. It is the genre of desire and the genre of rebellion, the literary mode of the Jacobite movement. In Flora's vision, the rebellion appears as the culminating moment in a plot from Gothic romance:

> She believed it the duty of her brother, of his clan, of every man in Britain, at whatever personal hazard, to contribute to the restoration which the partizans of the Chevalier de St. George had not ceased to hope for.   (ch. 21; 212)

The aim of the rebellion is to defeat the usurping Elector of Hanover and to restore the rightful monarch to his throne. Flora serves as a propagandist for the Jacobite cause. A true believer in the rightness of the movement, she becomes an enchanting ideologue, an apologist for the rebellion who uses the conventions of romance to ratify the actions of the rebels. In her seduction of Waverley, she proclaims the virtues of the Stuart line in the language and rhythm of ballad, singing the glories of the ancient Scottish past and reviving memories of old Scotland's heroes.

Waverley's romantic imagination is the crucial element of his attraction to Flora. He goes to hear Flora sing an ancient Highland song "like a knight of romance ... conducted by the fair Highland damsel, his silent guide." The glen into which he is led "seemed to open into the land of romance":

> The rocks assumed a thousand peculiar and varied forms. In one place, a crag of huge size presented its gigantic bulk, as if to forbid the passenger's farther progress ... At a short turning, the path ... suddenly placed Waverley in front of a romantic waterfall ... The borders of this romantic reservoir corresponded in beauty, but it was a beauty of stern and commanding cast, as if in the act of expanding into grandeur. Mossy banks of turf were broken and interrupted by huge fragments of rock, and decorated with trees and shrubs, some of which had been planted under the direction of Flora, they added to the grace, without diminishing the romantic wildness of the scene.   (ch. 22; 222–24)

Waverley's meeting with Flora within the frame of this "romantic" scene inspires his courtship of her. But the scene appears within a

theatrical context arranged by Scott so as to create a distance between
the perceptions of the character and the tone of the narrator. Scott
wants to remind us of Waverley's aesthetic predisposition in this
passage and to suggest at the same time that the effect of the scene
on Waverley is the result of contrivance, of artistic arrangement
working on an imagination shaped by an education in romance.
Waverley's fancy is typically active here, rendering Flora's maid as
a "fair Highland damsel." But the artist behind the scene at the
waterfall is Flora, who has "decorated" the area with trees and shrubs
and chosen the waterfall as the "appropriate accompaniment" for
her Highland song.

In contrast to the gentle and fair-haired Rose, Flora is precisely
the figure to capture Waverley's imagination. Gazing on the waterfall
to which she has lured her guest, Flora appears to Waverley "like one
of those lovely forms which decorate the landscapes of Poussin." The
wild beauty of the place encourages his sense of "delight and awe,"
and he compares Flora once again to a figure from literature, "a fair
enchantress of Boiardo or Ariosto" (ch. 22; 224–25). The third-
person perspective employed here establishes a firm distinction
between narrator and character, which, in turn, emphasizes the
disjunction between fiction and reality which Scott repeatedly asserts:
"Even in her hours of gaiety, she was in his fancy exalted above the
ordinary daughters of Eve, and seemed only to stoop for an instant
to those topics of amusement and gallantry which others appear to
live for" (ch. 24; 239).

The issue of Scott's attitude toward Waverley's imaginative
transformations is a crucial one. Scott appears at certain key moments
to distinguish his narrator sharply from his hero, and to recommend
a rational and realistic vision to his reader. But to neglect Scott's
transformations of history is to ignore one of the novel's most
significant political motives. Romance serves in *Waverley* as both a
way of escaping history and of domesticating a threatening past.
Waverley's trip to Tully-Veolan is not only an escape from the rigors
of military life, but from social and political responsibility. In the
neighborhood of Dundee where his regiment was quartered, the dis-
affected gentry had shown little hospitality to the occupying British
forces, and the townspeople, "chiefly engaged in mercantile pursuits,
were not such as Waverley chose to associate with" (ch. 7; 70). But
in the Baron's house Waverley can momentarily divest himself of his

military rank and his duties as a functionary of the British army and simply be a guest. The environs of Tully-Veolan encourage the imaginative propensities which were suppressed by the regimen of military life and provide him with numerous objects and events on which his fancy can do its work.

By representing the Highlands from the romantic perspective of his hero, Scott gives the reader a means of evading the novel's presentations of "real history." Scott does not overtly endorse Waverley's vision of things. Yet it is Waverley's vision against which the novel's realism is defined. Scott gives us a dual vision of history, and for much of the novel we are obliged to see double. The effect of the distant perspective and the picturesque rendering of the landscape is consistently countered by the "philosophical" view of Scott's narrator. What we read in the most prominent scenes of the novel is a contest for the terms of perception, for the aesthetic and epistemological high ground from which the past is to be perceived and rendered.

The borderline between the realms of "romance" and "real history" is drawn early in *Waverley* and underlined repeatedly. The realm of romance is one of dreams. At his meeting with Flora in her glen, Waverley feels he has "never, even in his wildest dreams, imagined a figure of such exquisite and interesting loveliness." On his first return to the south, Waverley makes a goddess of Flora:

All that was commonplace, all that belonged to the everyday world, was melted away and obliterated in these dreams of imagination, which only remembered with advantage the points of grace and dignity that distinguished Flora from the generality of her sex ... (ch. 29; 297)

This verbal link between Waverley's imaginative activity and dreaming is made explicit at numerous points in the novel.[11] As Waverley awaits passage to the cave of Donald Bean Lean, he has "time to give himself up to the full romance of his situation." About to visit the hideout of a cattle-thief, he is "wrapt in the dreams of imagination." The only drawback for Waverley is "the cause of the journey," the theft of the Baron's milk-cows. But this bit of "real history" is of little importance to him at this moment, and he keeps "this degrading incident ... in the background" (ch. 16; 167). In relegating the theft to the "background," Waverley avoids the political conflict which Scott describes as the root cause of the creagh. Fergus MacIvor has profited by running a sort of protection racket, collecting fees from

estates near the Highland line in return for regulating the activities
of the bandits who use his territory as a haven. When the Baron halted
the payments as a point of honor, Fergus withdrew his protection
from Tully-Veolan; hence the theft of the Baron's livestock. But
Waverley refuses to let the sordid circumstances leading up to his
journey spoil the romantic possibilities of his meeting with the bandit.
His dreaming sets the struggle between two declining social orders
momentarily aside, making history a backdrop for romance and a
pretext for experiencing the novelty and danger of an excursion into
the Highlands.

Romance is an instrument of wish-fulfillment in *Waverley*, a form
through which the hero can project his desire onto an external world
and evade, at least momentarily, the effects of the political struggle
which goes on around him. Waverley is not merely transforming the
external world on his trip to the Highlands, but reproducing the world
of Waverley-Honour, in which courtship and warfare were a source
of pleasure which had no consequences in the world outside of the
mind, in which action was a figment of his fancy. In his courtship
of Flora, Waverley once again engages in the "castle-building" which
was his primary occupation in the shelter of his uncle's mansion.
Waverley's perception of Flora is, Scott tells us, a result of physical
distance from the object of his desire. Yet Scott's leisurely discussion
of the effects of distance on perception applies equally to his own
techniques of presentation:

Distance, in truth, produces in idea the same effect as in real perspective.
Objects are softened, and rounded, and rendered doubly graceful; the harsher
and more ordinary points of character are mellowed down, and those by which
it is remembered are the more striking outlines that mark sublimity, grace
or beauty. There are mists too in the mental as well as the natural horizon,
to conceal what is less pleasing in distant objects, and there are happy lights
to stream in full glory upon those points which can profit by brilliant
illumination.   (ch. 29; 296)

Waverley itself is a means of achieving this effect of distance. It is
for Scott a fiction which allows him to revise history, to recast things
in such a way as to establish a transhistorical perspective in the present.
The novel is Scott's own daydream of history. By setting the threat
of political subversion in the temporal position of several decades past,
Scott accomplishes the softening and rounding of figures and events,
the graceful rendering, the mellowing which he describes as the

products of distance. Scott was led to his own "castle-building" not only by his sympathy for the ways of the past, but by his belief in the merits of the present order, in the value of stability and prosperity. The suppression of the Jacobite rebellion and the subsequent pacification of the Highlands was, in Scott's view, a job well done. Scott revives the spirit of rebellion so that it can be properly laid to rest, so that its excesses might be committed in dignified fashion to the obscurity of a heroic age that had passed some "sixty years since."

It is not enough, then, to say that Scott viewed British history in two divergent ways, that he was of two minds, and that this explains the mixed modes of *Waverley* and the other Scottish novels. The most significant ambivalence of *Waverley* lies not in Scott's dualistic vision of history, but in his sense of his purpose in writing historical novels, and in his conception, implicitly expressed, of the power and limits of fictional language. *Waverley* is a conscious effort to resist the very historical forces which Scott claims to represent. While Scott regarded romance as a distortion of history, he saw it at the same time as a powerful instrument for rewriting the past. The formal consequences of this ideological tension are visible in the generic shifts which occur repeatedly in the novel. Standing on a "small, craggy eminence," Waverley views the Highland army on its way to England. His view from the promontory yields a "singular and animating prospect":

At length the mixed and wavering multitude arranged themselves into a narrow and dusky column of great length, stretching through the whole extent of the valley. In the front of the column the standard of the chevalier was displayed, bearing a red cross upon a white ground, with the motto Tandem Triumphans ... Many horsemen of this body ... added to the liveliness, though by no means to the regularity, of the scene, by galloping their horses as fast forward as the press would permit, to join their proper station in the van ... The irregular appearance and vanishing of these small parties of horsemen, as well as the confusion occasioned by those who endeavoured, though generally without effect, to press to the front through the crowd of Highlanders, maugre their curses, oaths, and opposition, added to the picturesque wildness what it took from the military regularity of the scene.

(ch. 44; 137–38)

A comically inflated explanation of the "irregular appearance and vanishing of the horsemen" is a reminder that this "remarkable spectacle" is, at least in part, a picturesque reworking of unheroic materials: "The fascinations of the Circes of the High Street and the potions of strength with which they had been drenched overnight, had probably detained these heroes within the walls of Edinburgh somewhat later than was consistent with their morning duty.''

The panoramic perspective thus produces a prospect combined of "picturesque wildness" and "military regularity" (ch. 44; 138). From his craggy eminence, Waverley watches the apparently "spontaneous and confused" motions of the Highlanders coalesce into "a pattern of order and regularity," to form a column that extends the entire length of the valley. The irregular movements of the straggling horsemen enhance the picturesqueness of the scene. Yet a "nearer view" of the column diminishes the powerful effect of the panoramic view. On a closer examination, Waverley can distinguish the specific ranks, military and social, of the men who make up the column: "The leading men of the clan were well-armed with broadsword, target, and fusee, to which all added the dirk, and most the steel pistol. But these consisted of gentlemen, that is, relations of the chief ..." Behind the vanguard are the "common peasantry" of the Highlands, poorly dressed and equipped, "worse-armed, half-naked, stinted in growth, and miserable in aspect." The column is filled out by these "Helots," men "forced into battle by the arbitrary authority of the chieftains," who march to the Prince's fight "very sparingly fed, ill-dressed, and worse-armed than their masters" (ch. 44; 139–40).

Scott's far–near shift in perspective, the movement from panoramic vista to close-up view, is a graphic illustration of his meditations on the palliative influence of distance: "Distance, in truth, produces in idea the same effect as in real perspective" (ch. 29; 296). Beauty is a product of distance, whether that distance is physical or imaginative in nature. A close-up look reveals the actual consti- tution of the Highland army, the condition of the men who fill the ranks behind the impressive martial facade of the gentry. From the heights above a plain near Preston, Waverley witnesses another "military spectacle," the formation of battle-lines by the opposing armies. The armies appear "like two gladiators in the arena, each meditating upon the mode of attacking their enemy" (ch. 46; 154). But Waverley's comfortable sense of distance breaks down with the approach of an English cavalry party. The horsemen come so near to the Highlanders' position that Waverley can recognize the standard of his old troop and the voice of his commanding officer. At this moment, the consequences of his position become clear to him:

It was at that instant, that, looking around him, he saw the wild dress and appearance of his Highland associates, heard their whispers in an uncouth and unknown language, looked upon his own dress, so unlike that which he had worn from his infancy, and wished to awake from what seemed at that moment a dream, strange, horrible, and unnatural. (ch. 45; 156)

Waverley now sees the dream for what it is, realizing the unreality of his life up to this instant. This moment of self-recognition will eventually lead him out of the land of "military and romantic adventure" and into the "reality" of the historical present. It is a turning point in Waverley's gradual movement back towards his native society, to the mid-eighteenth-century England from which he has been a fugitive. Hereafter, Waverley's development is described as the process of awakening from a dream. The changes he undergoes are presented as an emergence from the fantasy-life which he had lived in his northern haven and his entry into a world which has "history" rather than legend and romance, a world which is dominated, not coincidentally, by English political and cultural values.

Following his rescue from captivity by Fergus's Highlanders, Waverley had become more deeply engaged in the world of romance than ever before. After saving him from the clutches of the radical Presbyterian Gilfillan, the Highlanders escort Waverley to a "fertile and romantic country" on the banks of a rapidly running river: "On the opposite bank of the river, and partly surrounded by a winding of its stream, stood a large and massive castle, the half-ruined turrets of which were already glittering in the first rays of the sun" (ch. 38; 78). Doune is presently a stronghold for the adherents of the Stuart cause. To Waverley, the castle is appealing for its aesthetic value as a "picturesque" structure (ch. 38; 79). In Scott's broader vision, the Gothic ruins of Doune are a singularly appropriate quarters for the rebel army.

At Holyrood castle, the current headquarters of the Prince, Waverley is led into "a long, low and ill-proportioned gallery" in which hang "the portraits of kings past." As the legendary home of the ancient Scottish monarchy, Holyrood is a fitting residence for a politician who justifies his claim to the throne by his purportedly direct relationship to the royal family. But Scott's comments on the portraits imply that the dynastic claims of the Stuarts are little more than a boldly asserted fiction. The pictures which hang in the guard-chamber to the Prince's apartments are "affirmed" to be the portraits of kings "who, if they ever flourished at all, lived several hundred years before the invention of painting in oil colors ..." (ch. 39; 92). These portraits of royalty are thus conjectural images of figures whose actual existence is a matter of doubt, as much pictures of legends as of real figures. Scott's larger suggestion is that Holyrood is a scene got up for purposes of propaganda. Fergus performs the function of the Prince's advance man, leading the impressionable Waverley to meet Charles Edward in the venerated home of the Scottish monarchy. Fergus knows very well how to manipulate Waverley by appealing to the young man's aesthetic predisposition. In manner and appearance, Charles Edward neatly fits Waverley's conception of the "hero of romance." Influenced by the personal solicitations of the Prince and the atmosphere of the "paternal palace" of the Stuarts, Waverley joins the cause. Kneeling to Charles Edward in accordance with an ancient ritual of fealty, Waverley devotes "heart and sword to the vindication of his rights!" (ch. 40; 96).

Scott's description of the Prince's gestures as "rather like a hero of romance than a calculating politician" (ch. 43; 124) betrays the artifice behind the scene at Holyrood. Warned by Scott's remarks on the paintings, we are prepared to read the Prince's conduct as a performance with specific political motives. In this instance, physical proximity has the effect of increasing Waverley's distance from hard political realities. The mists produced by Waverley's romantic imagination make him susceptible to Fergus's manipulations and to the Prince's deliberate courting of his familial prejudices in favor of the Stuarts. While Scott separates himself from his excessively credulous hero, he conveys in the scene of Waverley's audience with the Prince his sense of the remarkable potency of historical fictions. The paintings on the wall of the guard-chamber constitute a genealogical story about the kings of Scotland, a story appropriated by Charles Edward in the very gesture of pitching his headquarters at Holyrood, which has thus become a part of the legitimizing strategy employed by the Jacobite leadership. Waverley's perception of the Prince as the rightful heir to the throne of Scotland and England doing battle with the usurper is founded in the same romance plot which gives meaning to the pictures in the gallery. The scenes at Holyrood, rife with hints of the fiction-making behind the Prince's political enterprise, make of Flora MacIvor's rationale for the rebellion a compelling dynastic myth.

The distancing artifice of the Prince's court at Holyrood conceals the deflating reality of Charles Edward's family history, the history which had earlier prompted Waverley to question the merits of the Jacobite cause. As Waverley considered his dilemma before returning south from Fergus's Highland stronghold, he remarked to himself that the forced abdication of James II was largely justified, and that the departure of the last Stuart monarch had been followed by years of "peace and glory" for Britain: "Reason asked, was it worthwhile to disturb a government so long settled and established and to plunge a kingdom into civil war, for the purpose of replacing upon the throne the descendants of a monarch by whom it had been willfully forfeited?" (ch. 28; 290). At Holyrood, art triumphs over "reason," and romance proves more powerful than "real history."

But Waverley's next meeting with Flora has the opposite effect of his meeting with the Prince. As he left the Highlands, Waverley's passion for Flora had grown. Distance had greatly improved the prospect. And now proximity has a deflating effect. Now the union he had longed for appears to him as a "day-dream" (ch. 43; 126), an illusion which has vanished abruptly in Flora's presence. In this encounter with Flora, Waverley becomes aware of his own "castle-building," of the fanciful nature of his conception of Flora. The cold reality of her presence forces him to recognize his vision of Flora as a trick of his imagination. But faced with the prospect of his failure with Flora, Waverley exerts his "powers of fancy, animation, and eloquence" (ch. 43; 130) to conceal his pain from the company. His response to Flora's cool rejection is to perform another kind of distancing, to create in his words and gestures the appearance of a gay composure which disguises his sense of wounded love and pride: "Distinguished by the favor of a Prince destined, he had room to hope, to play a conspicuous part in the revolution which awaited a mighty kingdom; excelling, probably, in mental acquirements ... could he, or ought he to droop beneath the frown of a capricious beauty?" (ch. 43; 128–29).

As Waverley revels in the company of the Prince, in the sense of upcoming battle, of his own importance in the movement, of his own gifts and acquirements, his desire is displaced from its sexual object into the channels of political and social ambition. Flora's coldness has the eventual effect not of depressing, but of arousing Waverley's powers of imagination. Thus stimulated, Waverley's ballroom artistry attracts "the general admiration of the company" (ch. 43; 130), including many of the ladies. But on the first real day of battle, Waverley perceives his relationship to the Highlanders in its fullest unreality. For Waverley, the battle of Prestonpan marks the beginning of his political disenchantment. Like his vision of a union with Flora, his position as a central figure in the ranks of the rebels now seems to him an illusion.

Waverley would seem to be a masterful work of fence-sitting, a nimble essay in British history which establishes at once the virtues of the past and the necessity of progress and successfully balances these two thematic imperatives in the marriage of Edward Waverley and Rose Bradwardine. But despite the reportorial tone of the "Postscript," Scott's position is no more neutral than that of Fergus MacIvor or Colonel Talbot. Now that the threat to public order is gone, Scott can well afford to admire both sides in the civil war. Scott knows that he has produced in the neat conclusion to his narrative a fiction of balance, that his relentlessly optimistic resolution to the novel's social and political conflicts has the same veridical value as the portrait of Fergus and Waverley which hangs in the dinner-parlour of the restored Tully-Veolan.

For Scott, the closing chapters of the narrative are no more real than Waverley's picturesque interpretations of the Scottish landscape in the early chapters. The only truth of the ending rests in Scott's elaboration of a social, political, and moral order in which he believed, a beneficent order in which the progress of the present is maintained while the virtues of the past are preserved and nurtured. This balancing act is managed in *Waverley* with an extraordinary skill, a degree of success which is seldom achieved in the other Scottish novels. Scott wrote *Waverley* not as a faithful account of the Jacobite rebellion as seen through the eyes of a representative Englishman, nor as a *Bildungsroman*, but as a fictive structure which permitted the projection and assimilation of a violent past. The end of Scott's strategies is to evoke a past that is colorful and dangerous, in which the members of a moribund social order act out the vices and virtues endemic to their historical moment, and to distance his hero from that past, preserving in the art of the novel what the hero must reject in order to survive.[12] *Waverley* destroys as it preserves; indeed, the novel destroys in order to preserve. *Waverley* reenacts the demise of the Jacobite movement, even as it celebrates the nobility of the clansmen and feudal lords who were an essential part of its political base. But the virtues of the old order become visible only from the temporal distance of "sixty years since."

Scott clearly recognized the necessary gap between historical reality and his own versions of the past, between the real and "reality effects."[13] In *Waverley*, he exploited this disjunction to promote his own vision of historical development. He used stories about past societies as a way of describing and justifying the changes he perceived to have occurred in England since the mid-eighteenth century. While Scott offers a version of British history which is sufficiently compelling to fool many critics, he reminds his reader repeatedly of the fictive nature of his own writing, as if to suggest that he, much like Waverley in his exchange with the Baron on the subject of history (chapter 13), is merely playing with the facts.

Scott's intentions in writing his "historical romances" were essentially benevolent. He was by no means a conscious propagandist for the Empire. Rather, he used stories about the past to ratify his own deeply held political convictions. Edward Waverley's "mastery of a spirit tamed by adversity" (ch. 60; 281) is made possible by the events in which he has participated. The Jacobite party has invaded England, and has, in turn, been repulsed and finally defeated by a superior British force. The defeat of the Highland army parallels Waverley's gaining of mastery over his wandering spirit. Only when the struggle between the British government and the recalcitrant Highlanders is over can Waverley take full possession of himself. Waverley's awakening from his dream is a process of re-anglicization. Yet the issue of achieving the right perception of things is as much a matter of aesthetic bias as of political correctness. The changes Scott makes in Edward Waverley have a generic corollary in Waverley's eschewal of romance for "real history," along with the epistemological implication of Waverley's recognition that his actions have hitherto been founded on romantic delusion. In *Waverley*, realism, artistic and philosophical, is the conqueror's way of seeing things, an anglicized mode of perception that can be assumed only after the war is over and the battle is won.

OLD MORTALITY: OLD EPITAPHS AND NEW STORIES

Scott's writing in *Waverley* is the fabrication of stories about a mythified past in the service of an ideologically biassed version of British history. His declared motive for writing in the "Postscript" to *Waverley* is one of "preserving some idea of the ancient manners of which I have witnessed the almost total extinction ..." This gesture of "preservation" is permitted by the "almost total extinction" of the old ways which he laments, with the appearance of sincerity, in the "Postscript." *Waverley* involves not only an effort at preservation, but a reenactment of the events that brought about the destruction of the Scottish feudal order. One of the greatest virtues of the Jacobite movement from the perspective of a prosperous early-nineteenth-century Briton is its decrepitude. Scott can mourn the demise of Jacobitism and the death of its greatest heroes because, in his time, a Stuart restoration could be no more than a sentimental fiction. It is from the relative security of sixty-odd years hence that Scott can speak of the '45 and the events that ensued from it in a tone of self-assurance. His purpose in *Waverley* is not only to preserve "ancient manners" in "imaginary scenes" (ch. 72; 402), but to make the past palatable to the reader of the present. He knows that in order to accomplish that task, he must transform the events of history as he knows it, lending to those events in the process a rightness and a dignity which are inherently lacking.

Scott uses the generic amalgam he labeled "historical romance" to tame what he perceived as a threatening past and to put a good face on the ugly historical prospect of the British conquest of the Highlands. By reminding the reader of the fictive character of his own work, Scott implicitly questions its historical value. In the same gesture, he undermines the seriousness of his historical subject. He makes light of history by rendering the past as an artistic convention that permits the indulgence of harmless sentiments.

Despite Scott's disclaimers of serious intent, the motive of his formal manipulations in *Waverley* is no less than a revision of history, the transformation of a bloody episode in the British conquest of the Highlands into a collection of sentimental stories and pictures. In *Old Mortality*, Scott's historical subject is again an abortive rebellion, the Covenanters' revolt of 1679. But here the suppression of rebellion, followed in *Waverley* by the gradual and peaceful displacement of the traditional order by the modern, issues in the destructive clashes of a protracted civil war, in a futile struggle between Whig and Royalist.

Scott's layered narrative structure does dual service,[14] restoring the crucial events of a violent past and placing the past at a comfortable distance in the framing chapters, raising the spectre of lower-class revolt so that it may be consigned to its final resting place. By evoking the figure of Robert Paterson, a real historical personage, in his own preface,[15] Scott sets before the reader a human token of Whig fanaticism. Scott's Paterson is a rebel whom history has deprived of his cause, a belated revolutionary who expresses his commitment to the principles of the Covenant in his tireless efforts to restore the epitaphs on the graves of the martyrs. His presence in the prefatory chapters works both as a memorial and a warning. Although by 1816 Old Mortality had long since joined the Whig martyrs, the spirit of revolt which he embodied was a vital force in Scott's time.[16]

Scott's purpose in connecting present with past through the figure of Old Mortality is to recall a series of crucial events in Scottish history and to mark thereby the presence of "Whiggery" in nineteenth-century Scotland. But the use of Peter Pattieson as an intermediary, as a collector and editor of disparate accounts of the past, works not only to correct the bias of Paterson's anecdotes, but to create still another refracting figure between the reader and real history. The past is finally available to the reader only through the triple mediation of Jedidiah Cleisbotham, Peter Pattieson, and Old Mortality. As a result of Scott's clever layering of narrators, Paterson's Whiggish version of the Covenanters' revolt becomes one source of material among others, one perspective, significant but limited, on the past.

At the close of his editorial introduction to "Tales of my Landlord," Jedidiah Cleisbotham disclaims responsibility for any inaccuracies in the narrative of Peter Pattieson, adding a cautionary note that Pattieson,

in arranging these tales for the press, hath more consulted his own fancy than the accuracy of the narrative; nay, that he hath sometimes blended two or three stories together for the mere grace of his plots. Of which infidelity, although I disapprove and enter my testimony against it, yet I have not taken upon me to correct the same, in respect it was the will of the deceased, that his manuscript should be submitted to the press without diminution or alteration. (*The Black Dwarf*, xxii)

Against Cleisbotham's disavowal, Chapter 1 of *Old Mortality*, Pattieson's "Preliminary," seems intended, at least in part, to establish the integrity of the narrator as an observer of the past. Pattieson emphasizes his scrupulous efforts to obtain sources of information which will serve to balance off the accounts of Old Mortality, and his aim of preserving a position of objectivity in presenting his narrative. Pattieson's express intention is to produce an "unbiassed picture of the manners of that unhappy period, and at the same time, to do justice to the merits of both parties" (ch. 1; 16). His information has been collected from a broad range of sources, from "packmen," "country weavers," and tailors to the descendants of "ancient and honourable families" loyal to the Stuart cause. While the anecdotal contributions of Old Mortality are his main source, Pattieson points out that he has taken considerable pains to "qualify" these tendentious narratives with reports from partisans of the other side:

> My readers will of course understand, that in embodying into one compressed narrative many of the anecdotes which I had the advantage of deriving from Old Mortality, I have been far from adopting either his style, his opinions, or even his facts, so far as they appear to have been distorted by party prejudice. I have endeavoured to correct or verify them from the most authentic sources of tradition, afforded by the representatives of either party.
> (ch. 1; 15).

Yet despite these assertions of neutrality, Pattieson's language suggests that he is more than merely a disinterested observer. Early in the "Preliminary" chapter, he describes the "charm" of an old burial-ground to which he walks as a respite from his labors as a schoolmaster. The source of the "charm" lies, in part, in the age of the graves and the absence of any mark of recent death, of "new" mortality:

> The monuments, of which there are not above seven or eight, are half-sunk in the ground, and overgrown with moss. No newly erected tomb disturbs the sober serenity of our reflections by reminding us of recent calamity, and no rank-springing grass forces upon our imagination the recollection, that it owes its dark luxuriance to the foul and festering remnants of mortality which ferment beneath. The daisy which sprinkles the sod, and the harebell which hangs over it, derive their pure nourishment from the dew of heaven, and their growth impresses us with no degrading or disgusting recollections. Death has indeed been here and its traces are before us; but they are softened

and deprived of their horror by our distance from the period when they have
been first impressed. (ch. 1; 4)

Temporal distance serves as a screen, concealing from the contemporary observer the "foul and festering remnants of mortality,"
permitting him to meditate on the dead simply as others who have
gone before, softening and mitigating the calamities of the past.
Distance is a source of protection and comfort for the living, a
palliative against death.

Within this place of respite, Pattieson meets Old Mortality himself,
"renewing" with his chisel the "half-defaced inscriptions" (ch. 1; 7)
on the tombstones of the Whig martyrs buried there. The labors of
Old Mortality militate against the effects of distance. Paterson's
purpose is to perpetuate the memory of the Cameronian brethren by
restoring their epitaphs, to remind future generations of their
martyrdom, and thereby to encourage their descendants to defend
the true religion. Within the full context of Scott's reflections on
the process of making art from artifact, Pattieson's corrections of
Old Mortality take on the status of defacements. The force of Old
Mortality's biassed accounts of the past is, like the work he performs
with his chisel, to make old mortality new, to revive the memory of
his fallen ancestors, to revitalize the old cause by preserving the last
written vestiges of its martyrs. In qualifying the Whig bias of Old
Mortality's stories with traditional sources, Pattieson's digging into
the past not only serves the end of ideological balance, but lays the
martyrs to rest once more among the daisy and harebell of the burial-
ground.

But while Pattieson promises to present an "unbiassed picture" of
the past, his essay in history lies at a double-remove from its subject.
Pattieson's work entails the correction of Old Mortality's anecdotes
with stories drawn from a "tradition" much broader socially and
politically than the primary material. "Tradition" for Pattieson
means simply the loose agglomeration of legend and fact related to
the "killing time" which has been transmitted informally over the
decades. Grounded as it is on the anecdotes of an old Cameronian,
whose accounts are already distorted by "party prejudice," Pattieson's
narrative can only be a correction of a previous distortion, a version
of the past blended from prior constructions. Against Old Mortality's
partisan account, Pattieson offers a narrative in which the past

appears as a conflict between two competing fanaticisms, with this conflict resolved not by the victory of one party over the other, but by the gradual passing of time. Jedidiah Cleisbotham's remark that Pattieson "hath more consulted his own fancy than the accuracy of the narrative" is worth recalling here. Just as Cleisbotham's editions are blended from Pattieson's tales, the world which is presented in Pattieson's narrative is, inescapably, a made world, "blended" from "two or three stories together." Thus framed, the narrative of *Old Mortality* becomes a transformation of twice-told tales. Pattieson's writing is a rechiseling of Paterson's work, a renovation which, although it is performed with the most respectful of intentions, involves a writing over of the old epitaphs with a new story of the past. With this new story, Scott seeks to overcome the distortions of the Whigs and their persecutors and to forge a position epistemologically superior to their mutually destructive fanaticisms.

The opening of the novel's main part seems to mark a sharp break from the metafictional musings of the prefatory chapters. Here, the work of framing is momentarily set aside. The figure of Pattieson practically disappears, and Old Mortality, Pattieson's primary source, is virtually invisible until the beginning of the last eight chapters. Scott appears to begin the historical narrative *in medias res*, leaping from a self-conscious discussion of his artistic procedures to a description of the political forces at play in the late Stuart period. This brief and general account of the tensions between the government and the dissident Presbyterians is contextual matter for Scott's depictions of a particular social ritual in an unnamed royal burgh in the Lowlands in May, 1679. But the move from metafiction to history is less abrupt than it appears. The dual preoccupations of the introductory chapters extend into the narrative itself.

The local wappen-schaw represents the imposition of a symbol of feudal power on a resistant social reality. Scott opens his narrative with an account of the attempts by the Stuart regime to revive feudal institutions during the Restoration as a counter to the "Puritanical" spirit of the late republican government. The government's efforts to restore the martial spirit of the wappen-schaw were actively opposed by the Presbyterian party. But despite the opposition, landholders were obliged to send their sons, tenants, and vassals in accordance with the size of the estate.[17] Even as her rents and retinue shrank, Lady Margaret Bellenden remained zealous in fulfilling her duty as vassal to the King. Scott's historical point is that with the decay of the feudal order in Scotland, the wappen-schaw is little more than an instrument for enforcing discipline among the lower classes, a trumped-up spectacle of aristocratic power. No longer an expression of real social relations, it is now an empty symbol, a form drawn from an obsolete social code and used in the interest of the royal regime.

The merits of the scene as a piece of historical realism have been amply praised, and there is no need to add another voice to the accolade.[18] What is often passed over in encomiums to the novelist's skills as a depictor is another, no less important, form of realism, the philosophical position that finds in the language of both sides a warped vision of history. Scott uses the wappen-schaw not only to reveal religious and political conflicts in the district, but to illustrate the party prejudices of Lady Margaret. The scene closes with a bit of comic satire on aristocratic values, as the halfwit Guse Gibbie, pressed into service in the absence of Cuddie Headrigg, is thrown from his horse and stripped of his ill-fitting buffcoat (ch. 2; 29). Scott's target here is the outmoded feudal perspective of Lady Margaret, who regards attendance at the wappen-schaw as an indispensable gesture of fealty to the King, and who is outraged at the exposure of the family's true condition.

Linked with Lady Margaret's humiliation at this minor misfortune is her repetition of the story of the King's "disjune" at Tillietudlem in the days of the civil war:

The personal retinue of Lady Margaret, on this eventful day, amounted only to two lackeys, with which diminished train she would on any other occasion have been much ashamed to appear in public. But for the cause of royalty, she was ready at any time to have made the most unreserved personal sacrifices. She had lost her husband and two promising sons in the civil wars of that unhappy period; but she had received her reward, for, on his route through the west of Scotland to meet Cromwell in the unfortunate field of Worcester, Charles the Second had actually breakfasted at the Tower of Tillietudlem; an incident which formed from that moment an important era in the life of Lady Margaret, who seldom afterwards partook of that meal without detailing the whole circumstance of the royal visit ...   (ch. 2; 27)

Scott allows Lady Margaret more than sufficient cause for supporting the Royalist party. Her birth, education, and the personal suffering she experienced at the hands of the King's enemies would explain her allegiances. But Scott's satire implies that what anchored her to the

Jacobite cause was not only these powerful historical and social determinants, but the force of a symbol – a simple and mundane gesture of royal favor:

> If Lady Margaret had not been a confirmed Royalist already, from sense of high birth, influence of education, and hatred to the opposite party, through whom she had suffered such domestic calamity, the having given a breakfast to majesty, and received the royal salute in return, were honours enough of themselves to unite her exclusively to the fortunes of the Stuarts.
>
> (ch. 2; 28)

Won over by these signs of favor, Lady Margaret repeats the story of the King's disjune at even the slightest occasion. The arrival of Claverhouse and Lord Evandale affords her a rough analogy for the visit of Charles, and once more she relives that brief but glorious moment. The repetition of the story takes on the force of an incantation, invoking a world in which the dignity and importance of the Bellenden family, severely diminished by the economic decline of the estate, is ratified by the royal salute. The world which she creates thereby shields her from the conflictual world of Scotland in 1679, where an arrogant monarchy barely restrained by its Parliament handles dissident subjects with brute military force. Her world is a Royalist daydream, a verbal world generated by the repeated retelling of an old story.

The debate between Lady Margaret and Mause Headrigg over Cuddie's absence from the retinue of Tillietudlem is a clash between two disparate verbal worlds, a skirmish between conflicting ideologies. Blinded by her zeal for observing ancient feudal customs and her jealous regard for the prestige of her family, Lady Margaret charges Mause with failing to perform her duties as a vassal:

> Is it true ... that you hae taen it upon you, contrary to the faith you owe to God and the King and to me, your natural lady and mistress, to keep back your son frae the wappen-schaw, held by the order of the sheriff, and to return his armour and abulyiements at a moment when it was impossible to find a suitable delegate in his stead, whereby the Barony of Tillietudlem, both in the person of its mistress and indwellers, has incurred sic a disgrace and dishonour as hasna befa'en the family since the days of Malcolm Canmore?
>
> (ch. 7; 93)

Provoked by these accusations of disloyalty, Mause fires a returning shot in the form of a Scriptural analogy. Drawing on the Old

Testament, she compares the wappen-schaw to the idolatry of Nebuchadnezzar. "Prelacy," Mause declaims, "is like the great golden image in the plain of Dura,"

and as … Shadrach, Meshach, and Abednego were borne out in refusing to bow down and worship, so neither shall Cuddie Headrigg, your ladyship's poor pleughman, at least wi' his auld mother's consent, make murgeons or Jenny-flections, as they ca' them, in the house of the prelates and curates, nor gird him with armor to fight in their cause, either at the sound of kettledrums, organs, bagpipes, or any kind of music whatever.

(ch. 7; 95–96)

The angry exchange between mistress and servant, ignited by Lady Margaret's indignation at the embarrassment of her retinue, quickly escalates beyond its original proportions as a domestic fracas into a full-scale argument over religious and political principles, with one absurd prejudice meeting its opposite head-on, and no possibility of reconciliation. Ignored in the fray is the simple and practical fact of Cuddie's presence at the popinjay contest in disguise, which renders the debate superfluous.

In his treatment of these relatively minor events, Scott establishes at once the terms of the conflict which the novel is designed to resolve and his narrator's position in relation to that conflict. The social basis of the struggle between the Whigs and the Royalists is grasped easily enough through Scott's explanations. More importantly, Scott thematizes in these scenes the distance between socially determined languages and historical reality, the idea that individuals are bound to read the events of their lives and the larger processes of history through the perceptual grid of their class prejudices. Scott not only exposes the feudal mystifications of which Lady Margaret is a victim, but unmasks the quasi-theological rhetoric of the Covenanters. Henry Morton's reservations about the Covenanters have to do not only with their radical principles, but with their Scriptural polemics, their exploitation of narratives from the Old Testament as the original versions of their own plight. The sermons of the Whig preachers after the battle of Drumclog are rendered as propaganda pieces, executed with varying degrees of skill by faithful adherents to the cause. Kettledrummle's efforts would have been "fastidiously rejected by an audience with any portion of taste" (ch. 18; 279). But Ephraim MacBriar's speech, though "not altogether untainted by the coarseness of his sect," succeeds by "the influence of good natural taste." MacBriar is a subtly skilled orator, a painterly master of his particular genre, whose use of Scriptural language yields "a rich and solemn effect, like that which is produced by a ray of sun streaming through the storied representations of saints and martyrs on the Gothic window of some ancient cathedral" (ch. 18; 279). MacBriar's art, grounded in Scriptural allusion, is an enriching transformation of ancient narratives. It is a revision of "storied representations," an interpretation of Biblical texts which becomes an allegory for the plight of the Covenanters, in which the events of the Old Testament are deftly conflated with those of the battle of Drumclog. The sermon elevates his audience, weary from the rigors of warfare, above the calamities of their earthly lives, dignifying their exertions with the authority of Holy Writ, and aligning their cause with the purposes of the Deity. It is a virtuoso performance which makes the story of the westland Whigs into the story of God's chosen people.

Scott's emphasis on MacBriar's artifice marks the sermon clearly as an elaborate picture of the past, an interpretation of history which transforms reality in the service of narrow sectarian interest. MacBriar is a Whig ideologue whose art works to justify the ways of God to his chosen people, to legitimize the violence of the rebels' actions and to unify the disparate religious and social factions which make up the Presbyterian party into a single body. To Scott, the powerful rhetoric of the Covenanters is a form of self-deception, like Lady Margaret's story of the King's disjune. It is a means of concealing the ugly truth of the rebels' brutality in battle, of patching over the factionalism that divides the Presbyterian interest, and of justifying the Whigs' intolerance for other religious and political creeds.

The figure of Burley illustrates the mystifying power of Presbyterian polemics. Although Burley is given in his speech to the Scripture-laden pronunciations of his covenanting brethren, it is the force of private ambition which drives him to seek an alliance with the moderate faction. In a short biographical sketch, Scott discovers in the rebel leader a deep strain of vice, a dark blot of sin which survived Burley's conversion:

Unfortunately, habits of excess and intemperance were more easily rooted out of his dark, saturnine, and enterprising spirit, than the vices of revenge and ambition, which continued, notwithstanding his religious professions, to exercise no small sway over his mind. Daring in design, precipitate and violent in execution, and going to the very extremity of the most rigid recusancy, it was his ambition to place himself at the head of the Presbyterian interest. (ch. 21; 7–8)

Beneath Burley's ardent professions of faith and commitment to his calling as a soldier of the true religion is a will to power. It is this force, inextricably mingled with his religious and political convictions, that drives Burley in his battle with the government. His rebellion against established authority is not the just resistance of an oppressed dissenter, but the private revolt of an "enterprising spirit" against the trammels of an inferior social and political position. Against the honest, though badly misguided, zeal of MacBriar, Burley's efforts to assemble the Presbyterian interest into a united front appear self-aggrandizing.

Burley's consciousness of his own position remains throughout that of a warrior fighting for the cause of the Master, constantly beset by the powers of darkness. But Morton's encounter with Burley in the Black Linn of Linklater demonstrates the self-deluding effect of Burley's religious professions. Hiding from the pursuit of government troops, Burley imagines himself doing battle with a "mortal enemy," thrusting his sword into the air and proclaiming victory over the foe (ch. 43; 317). With this unconscious fit of shadow-boxing, Scott writes off Burley as a victim of his own "heated and enthusiastic imagination" (ch. 43; 318), a maniac who grapples with his own vices under the delusion that he is wrestling with the powers of Evil.

Burley's counterpart on the Royalist side is no less deluded. Claverhouse is given to a more genteel form of delusion, to the perpetuation of the obsolete values of the chivalric code. While he openly admits his affinity with Burley – "You are right ... we are both fanatics" – Claverhouse justifies his fanaticism on the grounds of "honour," distinguishing this elevated principle from the "dark and sullen superstition" that moves his enemies. There is an essential distinction, Claverhouse believes, between the victims of his violence and those of the Whigs, between "the blood of learned and reverend prelates and scholars, of gallant soldiers and noble gentlemen, and the red puddle that stagnates in the veins of psalm-singing mechanics, crack-brained demagogues, and sullen boors ..." (ch. 35; 195). Against Morton's assertions of the equal value of all human life,

the aristocratic Claverhouse declares unashamedly that the value of
a life is directly proportional to the social status of the victim, that
the death of a mechanic is insignificant next to the death of an
archbishop. Claverhouse's contempt for "psalm-singing mechanics"
is linked with his fondness for the literature of chivalry, especially
the writings of Froissart, which he recommends to Morton. The pages
of Froissart are a source of inspiration superior even to "poetry
itself," a Bible of chivalry for the "high-born" devotee:

With what true chivalrous feeling he confines his expression of sorrow to the
death of the gallant and high-bred knight, of whom it was a pity to see the
fall, such was his loyalty to his king, pure faith to his religion, hardihood
toward his enemy, and fidelity to his lady-love! ... But, truly, for sweeping
from the face of the earth some few hundreds of villain churls, who are born
but to plow it, the high-born and inquisitive historian has marvellous little
sympathy ...   (ch. 35; 196)

Alongside his account of the events surrounding Drumclog and
Bothwell Bridge, Scott renders a series of demonstrably biassed
interpretations of these events, set off by Morton's criticism of both
parties to the conflict. Morton's language serves as a standard of
clarity, a criterion of moderation against which the wild flourishes
of the Covenanters can be measured and rejected as falsehoods, and
Claverhouse's hatred for his victims revealed as vicious snobbism.
But even Morton's vision is tainted with a kind of party prejudice.
His most significant emotional ties are with a woman from an old
landed family. He engages with relative comfort in the aristocratic
games of the popinjay and discourses more easily with the likes of
Claverhouse and Evandale than with the members of the oppressed
party whose standard he bears. While he claims to speak for his
downtrodden countrymen against the depredations visited upon them
by the London regime, his own speech is free of any traces of Lowland
vernacular.

Despite his temperate rhetoric, Morton's perceptions are prone to
distortion. His declaration of skepticism to Burley and MacBriar is
a blunt exposé of the Covenanters' polemics:

I will own frankly, Mr. Balfour ... much of this sort of language, which is
so powerful with others, is entirely lost on me ... I revere the Scriptures as
deeply as you or any Christian can do. I look into them with humble hope
of extracting a rule of conduct and a law of salvation. But I expect to find

this by an examination of their general tenor, and of the spirit which they uniformly breathe, and not by wresting particular passages from their context or by the application of Scriptural phrases to circumstances and events with which they have often very slender relation. (ch. 21; 4)

The kind of reading Morton rejects here is a more dangerous form of Mause Headrigg's comparison of the wappen-schaw to the idolatry of Nebuchadnezzar. In the instance of MacBriar's sermon, the failure to discriminate between Old Testament stories and real history is a destructive delusion, a blindness which leads to bloody and futile confrontation with the forces of a ruthless oppressor.

But in a dialogue with the pragmatic Cuddie, Morton engages in the very hermeneutic activity of which he accuses the Covenanters:

"I will resist any authority on earth," said Morton, "that invades tyrannically my chartered rights as a freeman; and I am determined I will not be unjustly dragged to a jail, or perhaps a gibbet, if I can possibly make any escape from these men either by address or force."

"Weel, that's just my mind too, aye supposing we hae a feasible opportunity o' breaking loose. But then ye speak o' a charter; now these are things that only belong to the like o' you that are a gentleman, and it mightna bear me through that am but a husbandman."

"The charter that I speak of," said Morton, "is common to the meanest Scotchman. It was that freedom from stripes and bondage which was claimed, as you may read in Scripture, by the Apostle Paul himself, and which every man who is freeborn is called upon to defend for his own sake and that of his countrymen."

"Hegh, sirs!" replied Cuddie, "it would hae been long or my Leddy Margaret, or my mither either, wad hae fund out sic a wise-like doctrine in the Bible ..." (ch. 14; 127)

Cuddie's praise of Morton's "wise-like doctrine" against the opinions of Lady Margaret and his mother reminds us that Morton has just performed his own act of Scriptural exegesis and application. Morton's is a mild, Erastian reading of a New Testament passage. Yet it is this same appropriation of Scriptural language and its use out of context for which Morton castigates Burley and MacBriar. Cuddie's doubts about the validity of the charter for a mere "husbandman" belie the real grounds of Morton's argument against government oppression. Precisely because he is a "gentleman," with the privileges attendant upon that position, Morton is free to regard the offenses committed against him as violations of his "chartered rights.'' The freedom to which Morton so confidently lays claim is in reality available not to "even the meanest of Scotchmen," but only to those of the upper orders. Morton thus speaks here not as a clear-eyed champion of universal rights, but as a moderate Presbyterian of the lower gentry, unconscious of his privileged position in the social hierarchy.[19]

In his perception of the obstacles to a union with Edith Bellenden, Morton is painfully conscious of the limitations attendant upon his own inferior social position. He fears losing Edith not because of any lack of feeling on her part, but because of "circumstances" beyond his power, the marked difference in their status:

Her situation was in every respect so superior to his own, her worth so eminent, her accomplishments so many, her face so beautiful, and her manners so bewitching, that he could not but entertain fears that some suitor more favored than himself by fortune, and more acceptable to Edith's family than he durst hope to be, might step in between him and the object of his affections.

(ch. 13; 202)

During his confinement at Tillietudlem, Morton's "cold fits" over Edith's return of his affections become an impelling force in his rebellion against the government. These crucial moments in Morton's "transformation" are not only an attempt by Scott to stitch together disparate levels of human life, but an effort as well to show how Morton's affections are bounded by his social experience, by his keen sense of the disparity between "her situation" and his own, and how, in turn, Morton's subjective life affects his decision to participate in the ongoing struggle.

At the opening of chapter 13, Scott emphasizes that the ensuing pages will deal with abstract relations and states of mind:[20]

To explain the deep effect which the few broken passages of the conversation we have detailed made upon the unfortunate prisoner by whom they were overheard, it is necessary to say something of his previous state of mind, and of the origin of his acquaintance with Edith.   (ch. 13; 199)

The explanation that follows is a study of Morton's character as it has been shaped by social and historical forces, by his family background, his broader experience outside of the family, and "the circumstances of the times." Morton's "diffidence and reserve," the emotional features that prevent him from straightforwardly declaring his interest in Edith, are a result of his acute sense of "dependence, of poverty, above all, of an imperfect and limited education." The conviction of his own social inferiority that results from these deprivations compels Morton to conceal his "talent and firmness of character" from all but his most intimate friends, and engenders the fear that he will lose Edith to a superior rival. In this state of mind, Morton is highly susceptible to any sign that Edith may have shifted her affections to a man of her own rank.

Morton's suspicions, Scott suggests, are grounded not on a lucid evaluation of Edith's real disposition towards him, but on his own predisposition to regard Edith as a superior being by virtue of birth and education, vulnerable to the charms of a suitor better favored than himself. Lord Evandale is a likely candidate:

Common rumour had raised up such a rival in Lord Evandale, whom birth, fortune, connections, and political principles, as well as his frequent visits at Tillietudlem, and his attendance upon Lady Bellenden and her niece at all public places, naturally pointed out as a candidate for her favour. It frequently and inevitably happened that engagements to which Lord Evandale was a party interfered with the meeting of the lovers, and Henry could not but mark that Edith either studiously avoided speaking of the young nobleman, or did so with obvious reserve and hesitation.   (ch. 13; 202)

While there are signs that might be interpreted as indications of Edith's preference for Morton's aristocratic rival, it is clear that such a reading is mistaken:

These symptoms, which in fact arose from the delicacy of her own feeling towards Morton himself, were misconstrued by his diffident temper, and the jealousy which they excited was fermented by the occasional observation of Jenny Dennison.   (ch. 13; 202–03)

Morton's conviction that he has lost Edith is the result of his inaccurate reading of "symptoms," his misconstruction of Edith's innocent "reserve and hesitation." It is the product of a mind whose range of perception is confined by a sense of its own inferiority, of a vision which is, like that of the novel's staunchest partisans, circumscribed by its own historical situation. Blinded by his conviction of his own inferiority, Morton interprets Edith's gestures as a silent expression of preference for a man of her own rank, when, in fact, Scott takes pains to observe, Edith pleads with Evandale out of an emotion which exceeds all social distinctions.

In explaining Morton's transformation as a response to the

perceived loss of Edith's affections, Scott performs a psychological reduction of political behavior. The "singular and instantaneous revolution in his character" which makes a rebel of Morton is instigated by his misapprehension of an innocent conversation:

The depth of despair to which his love and fortunes were reduced, the peril in which his life appeared to stand, the transference of Edith's affections, her intercession in his favour, which rendered her fickleness yet more galling, seemed to destroy every feeling for which he had hitherto lived, but at the same time awakened those which had hitherto been smothered by passions more gentle, though more selfish. Desperate himself, he determined to support the rights of his country, insulted in his person.   (ch. 13; 207)

Although Morton's protestations against the persecution practiced by the government are principled, he arrives at the point of despair only after learning of Edith's intercession and witnessing her colloquy with Evandale. In a fit of baseless jealousy, Morton forges a linkage between love and politics:

"And to what do I owe it," he said, "that I cannot stand up like a man and plead my interest in her ere I am thus cheated out of it? – to what but the all-pervading and accursed tyranny which afflicts at once our bodies, souls, estates, and affections? And is it to one of the pensioned cut-throats of this oppressive government that I must yield my pretensions to Edith Bellenden? I will not by Heaven! – It is a just punishment on me for being dead to public wrongs that they have visited me with their injuries in a point where they can least be brooked or borne."   (ch. 13; 205)

Scott leaves no doubt that the political offenses against Morton and his countrymen are real. But Morton's despair at the failure of his love is a result of his misapprehension. And this ill-founded emotion feeds his resentment towards the government. While Morton makes a plausible interpretation of the events leading up to his pardon, his reading nonetheless involves the imposition of political value on a series of incidents of which the real meaning is beyond the socially delimited range of his comprehension.

Within the narrative, Henry Morton stands in the same relation to the opposing sides as Pattieson to his sources.[21] Committed neither to one side nor the other, finding merit and fault on both sides equally, Morton is, like his counterpart in *Waverley*, a key prop in Scott's elaborate balancing act, a figure in which opposing ideologies can be accommodated. In contrast to the largely passive Edward

Waverley, Morton is given an active role in the struggle. Scott makes of his hero in *Old Mortality* an artist of compromise, seeking to establish a political center in which the antagonistic interests embodied in Burley and Claverhouse can be reconciled.

Yet despite his awareness that the past he presents in his novels is fictive, Scott persisted in writing as if historical omniscience were possible, as if he believed that he could somehow grasp the truth of the past in the language of his fiction. The Whig and Royalist versions of the past distort because each of the warring parties insists on the primacy of its own version of events, each puts forth its own partial account as complete and authoritative. In correcting the accounts of the combatants, Scott wanted to give his readers an impartial view of history and a corollary language in which that view could be rendered. Morton is Scott's solution to a problem, at once aesthetic and epistemological. The neutral party in a world dominated by conflict, Morton is invested not only with a perspective seemingly balanced but with a conception of language that appears to transcend the narrow polemics of both sides.

Against the class struggles that arose in the post-war years, Scott created a social structure in which the extremes of right and left could be reduced to the harmless relics of a colorful past. Scott attempted to impose order on a violent past by inserting into his depiction of the crisis a hero of appropriately mixed allegiances. The hero of *Old Mortality* is, like his creator, a political artist. Morton is a self-appointed diplomatist, seeking to forge a compromise between competing fanaticisms, to create a happy resolution to the tensions which have divided Scotland. Morton's professions of universal tolerance and his modest protests against the fanaticisms of both sides constitute a fiction of moderation within the novel's historical narrative, a structure within which the forces of revolt and reaction can be subsumed and rendered harmless. But Morton's efforts at diplomacy end in failure. The conflict which he tries so earnestly to resolve exceeds the ordering procedures of his proposed compromise and the unifying force of Scott's elaborate balancing act.

If Morton's moderate vision is contaminated, then by implication the "unbiassed" picture of the past promised by Peter Pattieson is an impossibility. Morton's petition to the Duke of Monmouth for "the redress of grievances" is, like the wappen-schaw prescribed by the Royalist government, an attempt to impose an anachronistic form on a discordant reality. Knowing the limits of his own strategies of compromise, Scott uses those limits as a way of disguising and ratifying his own vision of the past.

The absence of a compelling resolution to the conflict described in the main part of the novel has long been the subject of critical complaint.[22] But much of the dissatisfaction with the final chapters arises from a misapprehension of their complicated relation to the novel's historical narrative.[23] Scott attempted in his endings to shape from the materials of literature and history fictions which would resolve the conflicts he had described in his narratives and create the image of a harmonious future beyond the moment of crisis. If a historical resolution had been Scott's aim, it would have been better accomplished with a detailed recapitulation of the causes and effects of the 1688 Revolution.[24] What he offers instead is a proclamation of fictionality. The novel's denouement must be regarded as an attempt to unify the materials presented in its main part by a declaration and a demonstration of the powers of the tale-teller. Chapter 37 opens with a relaxed disquisition by Scott's narrator on the freedom of "tale-tellers" to dispense with the conventions which constrain theatrical writers:

It is fortunate for tale-tellers that they are not tied down like theatrical writers to the unities of time and place, but may conduct their personages to Athens and Thebes at their pleasure, and bring them back at their convenience. Time, to use Rosalind's simile, has hitherto paced with the hero of our tale; for, betwixt Morton's first appearance as a competitor for the popinjay and his final departure for Holland, hardly two months elapsed. Years, however, glided away, ere we find it possible to resume the thread of our narrative, and Time must be held to have galloped over the interval. Craving, therefore, the privilege of my cast, I entreat the reader's attention to the continuation of the narrative, as it starts from a new era, being the year immediately subsequent to the British Revolution.   (ch. 37; 222)

These casual observations on the relative laxity of the tale's conventions serve not only to solve the basic technical difficulty of a sharp break in chronology, but to remind the reader of Scott's role as artificer, as the manipulator of character and setting whose often whimsical mind produced the preceding narrative. Scott's solution to the destructive pattern of revolt and reaction is an abbreviated romance in which the conflicts elaborated in the main part of the novel can be brought to a conclusion. His unabashed assertion of the powers of the "tale-teller" calls into question the credibility of the narrator as a source of knowledge about the past, undermining the harsh reality effect of the historical narrative. But, more importantly, the opening lines of the chapter shift the novel's action and setting into another world. Scott has clearly set aside history here in favor of fiction, inserting his narrative persona into the lines of the novel to announce the inception of a new verbal world, the realm of the "tale-teller."[25] In this new world, a resolution to the unhappy sequence of events which led to Henry Morton's expatriation appears possible. The principal human agents in the narrative are brought back together in order, apparently, that matters may be set right.

Morton returns to his homeland just after the Glorious Revolution, during a period which is, the taleteller claims, one of relative repose after the turmoils brought about by the change of dynasty. Under the "prudent tolerance" of King William, the moderate changes in civil and religious government which Morton had bargained for before Bothwell Bridge have been enacted. History, and the tricks of the taleteller, have done what Henry Morton had failed to accomplish with his petitions:

> The triumphant Whigs, while they reestablished Presbytery as the national religion, and assigned to the General Assemblies of the Kirk their natural influence, were very far from going to the lengths which the Cameronians and the more extravagant portion of the nonconformists under Charles and James loudly demanded ... Those who had expected to find in King William a zealous convenanted monarch were grievously disappointed when he intimated his intention to tolerate all forms of religion consistent with the safety of the state. (ch. 37; 223–24)

Time has turned the tables, and the Jacobites, now the "undermost" party in Scotland, are driven to expedients once practiced by the radical Whigs, holding private meetings and forming secret societies for the preservation of their cause. The agitations of "the more violent party," the Presbyterian zealots dissatisfied with the arrangements made by King William, are undermined by lenient government policies toward dissenters. In the absence of official persecution, the ardor of the radical Whigs has gradually diminished, and they have "sunk into the scattered remnants of serious, scrupulous, and harmless enthusiasts of whom Old Mortality, whose legends," Peter Pattieson reminds us, "have afforded the groundwork of my tale, may be taken as no bad representative." The reference to Old Mortality is reassuring in its suggestion that the source of Pattieson's narrative was, after all, merely a remnant of the "violent party" which had routed the King's troops at Drumclog. Comforting though it may be, the fact that Robert Paterson was not "one of those" does not mitigate the threat posed by the Cameronian party in 1690, when the sect is still "strong in numbers and vehement in their political opinions ..." (ch. 37; 224–25).

Scott's design is, on the one hand, to make his story palatable to his reader by dismissing Old Mortality as a harmless enthusiast and, on the other, to remind his reader that, in 1690, the danger posed by the radical Whigs was not to be taken lightly. Scott has it both ways, calling attention to the threat of lower-class rebellion and setting that threat at a temporal distance from the compositional present. To the reader fearful at the prospect of rebellion, Scott offers the tacit assurance that his narrative of Drumclog and Bothwell is only a fiction grounded in Paterson's "legends," and not a veridical account of the lives of real individuals in history.

This brief and hazy description of political conditions in Scotland becomes a backdrop to what Welsh called the "romance" of the novel.[26] A shift in mode from history to romance is quietly signaled in the view of the former battlefield at Bothwell. Opposite the "romantic ruins of Bothwell Castle," the battlefield,

once the scene of slaughter and conflict, now lay as placid and quiet as the surface of a summer lake. The trees and bushes, which grew around in romantic variation of shade, were hardly seen to stir under the influence. The very murmur of the river seemed to soften itself into unison with the stillness of the scene around.   (ch. 37; 226)

At work here is one of Scott's favored techniques for retouching the conflicts he describes in his fiction, the strategy practiced and explicitly thematized in *Waverley*. Through the "romantic" view of things, the novel rehearses and announces the pacification of the landscape. In bringing the mode of romance to bear on Bothwell, Scott performs a painterly reworking of his own story, a production of his own production of history. Under the license of the taleteller, Scott engages in the mystifications with which he closed the narrative of *Waverley*, viewing the scene of a bloody struggle through the screen of romance.

The description of the cottage and environs which follows closely on the view of Bothwell enforces the effect of tranquility which Scott sought to create in his retrospective view of the battlefield. Scott's portrayal of peasant life is a deliberately artificial assertion of prosperous peace against the conflict which had raged in that very locale only a decade before:

The hut seemed comfortable, and more neatly arranged than is usual in Scotland. It had its little garden, where some fruit-trees and bushes were mingled with kitchen herbs; a cow and six sheep fed in a paddock hard by; the cock strutted and crowed, and summoned his family around him before the door; a heap of brushwood and turf, neatly made up, indicated that the winter fuel was provided; and the thin blue smoke which ascended from the straw brown chimney, and wended slowly out from among the green trees, showed that the evening meal was in the act of being made ready. To complete the little scene of rural peace and comfort, a girl of about five years was fetching water in a pitcher from a beautiful fountain of the purest transparency, which bubbled up at the root of a decayed oak tree, about twenty yards from the end of the cottage. (ch. 37; 227)

These images of peasant prosperity engender an illusion of "peace and comfort" that conceals the preconditions of Cuddie Headrigg's happy lot and diverts attention further away from the turbulent past toward a still and placid present. That this present is fictive in nature is quietly indicated by Scott's self-reflexive reference to his description as a "scene of rural peace and comfort." In Morton's dialogue with Cuddie, Scott calls into question the scene's assertion of beneficent order. Cuddie describes "the state of the country" in a bluff and confident tone:

Ou, the country's weel eneugh, an it werena that dour deevil Claver'se (they ca' him Dundee now) that's stirring about yet in the Highlands ... to set things asteer again, now we hae gotten them a' reasonably well settled. But Mackay will pit him down, there's little doubt o' that; he'll gie him his fairing, I'll be caution for it. (ch. 37; 228)

But as Cuddie turns from the present to the past, his story belies the substantiality of the scene over which he presides:

"You seem," said the stranger, "to live in a rich peaceful country."
"It's no to compleen o', sir, and we get the crop weel in," quoth Cuddie; "but if ye had seen the bluid rinnin' as fast on the tap of that brig yonder as ever the water ran below it, yet wadna hae thought it so bonny a spectacle."
(ch. 37; 228)

Cuddie's hyperbolic simile is a token of the "killing-time," which places before the reader, as before the sight of "the stranger," a striking reminder of the violence and bloodshed which dominated the view of Bothwell on that distant day.

The self-mocking gestures Scott makes repeatedly in the closing chapters preclude the possibility of a satisfying fiction of resolution. In the battle that ensues from the plot against Evandale, Scott disposes of Morton's chief rival for the hand of Edith Bellenden, dispatches Basil Olifant, the insidious turncoat and usurper of property rights, and arranges for the death of the fanatic Burley, all in the matter of a few pages. Cuddie's fortunate piece of marksmanship eliminates the main obstruction to the Bellendens' restoration in a single stroke. Olifant is a kind of anti-Burke, one of those active and grasping seekers after real estate who is duly punished at the end of the novel for his crimes against the institution of property. His alliance with Burley against Evandale marks him as an enemy of landed property and links his opportunism with the lower-class rebellion of which Burley is the instigator. Evandale's dying act is to join together the hands of Henry Morton and Edith Bellenden, a melodramatic gesture which both signals and sanctions the reunion of lovers parted by civil strife and self-delusion (ch. 44; 336–39).

But the unabashed trickery of the scene is insufficient as a way of bringing together the threads unraveled by the movement of history. It seems a mere formal necessity, a strategy for taking care of unfinished business, of dispatching this figure and that, of reuniting the hero with the heroine. These deficiencies are taken up by Pattieson in the novel's final chapter, in his presumably "unbiassed" account of tea with Miss Martha Buskbody. In her expectation of a happy resolution, Miss Buskbody ignores the historical value of Pattieson's narrative. But Miss Buskbody's sentimental revision simply repeats Scott's own interpretation of Pattieson's narrative in the novel's last eight chapters. The denouement is itself an attempt to project a more felicitous future than was promised by Morton's exile from Scotland.

Taken as part of the novel's framing apparatus, the final chapters can be seen as an elaboration and an enactment of Scott's reflections on the possibility of faithfully representing history in his fiction, and on the more immediate issue of how history is presented in *Old Mortality*. But to regard the novel as an extended essay in metafiction which uses history as its ostensible subject, but which has as its real motive a meditation on the process of making historical fictions, is to neglect one of the central features of Scott's writing about the past. Not only within the framing chapters, but within the main part of the novel, we find inscribed the writer's awareness that he is merely making pictures of the past, conjuring up verisimilitudinous illusions out of old stories, countered by an implicit claim to historical veracity.

The ironical distance engendered by the prefatory chapters undermines the credibility of the narrative, working thereby to separate the reader from the terrors of the past. Cleisbotham's criticism of Pattieson in the editor's "Introduction" to the Tales leaves the reader with the dilemma of either suspecting the reliability of Scott's narrator or of doubting the claims of both editor and narrator. In the figure of Morton, Scott holds out the possibility of a compromise between the novel's opposed fanaticisms. But his mocking treatment of the self-deceiving language of the combatants reduces the struggle between Whig and Royalist to a confrontation between two historical fictions, both equally deluded.

In Pattieson's narrative, there is no single, authoritative version of the past, only disparate stories projected by the opposing sides. Scott proposes a perspective that will transcend the destructive opposition of Whig and Royalist. With the story he has blended, he hopes to overcome the distortions in which the warring parties have entrapped themselves, and to forge a position from which he can bring the conflict to a felicitous conclusion. Editor and author of historical fictions, he seeks this position knowing that he is actually constructing it in the process of narrating a rebellion, conscious that he has produced a version of the past through the fiction of omniscient narration.

3

HISTORICAL FABLE AND POLITICAL FANTASY: *THE HEART OF MIDLOTHIAN* AND *THE BRIDE OF LAMMERMOOR*

THE HEART OF MIDLOTHIAN: REVISION AND REFORM

The conscious focus of *The Heart of Midlothian* is mainly on the reform of the existing social and political order. While the novel contains the rudiments of a moral and psychological study, it is also unabashedly topical. Scott is concerned here with the issue of the Union, with the troubled relationship between England and her Scottish subjects, and with the necessity of preserving Scotland's national identity within what he perceived as the essentially beneficial strictures of the Union settlement. The novel's generic tensions must be understood as a product of Scott's effort to write an ambitious political fable. Scott's resolution to the social and political conflicts he describes in *Midlothian* is to return the Scottish nation to the footing of a simple morality, founded on the social structure of the old peasantry. His solution to the formal and thematic dislocations which so many critics have hit upon is to write an extended piece of pastoral embellished with historical detail.

The discontinuity between the chapters following Jeanie Deans's audience with the Queen and the earlier sections of the novel dealing with the urban world of Edinburgh is particularly pronounced. As Scott brings Jeanie Deans within view of her new home at Knocktarlitie, he announces, somewhat ostentatiously, a change in mode.[1] A long quotation from Alexander Ross's "Fortunate Shepherdess" is followed by a description of Knocktarlitie which signals the character of the transition: "They landed in this Highland Arcadia, at the mouth of a small stream which watered the delightful and peaceable valley" (ch. 44; 313). Despite the undeniable formal disparity, the Knocktarlitie pastoral is not wholly unprepared for.

62

Jeanie Deans's journey to England and return to Scotland are framed in pastoral images. As she departs for London, Jeanie gazes back toward Woodend and Beersheba and thinks wistfully of her childhood:

On looking to the eastward down a prattling brook ... she could see the cottages of Woodend and Beersheba, the haunts and habitation of her early life, and could distinguish the common on which she had so often herded sheep, and the rivulet where she had pulled rushes with Butler, to plait crowns and sceptres for her sister Effie, then a beautiful but spoiled child, of about three years old.

Jeanie's backward glance yields an image of a simpler and better life, a verdant world of innocent and harmonious play untouched by the destructive forces of history. This is a passing glimpse of life before "the change of market days" (ch. 27; 21), of the condition of happy intimacy between the Deanses and Butlers which had existed before Effie's seduction. This vision of a better world, repeated at key points in the novel, serves as a counterweight to the turbulent and conflict-ridden scenes of urban life which dominate the novel's opening chapters.

As she is about to embark on her journey back to Scotland, Jeanie imagines to herself the good life which awaits the two families. In a rare and untypical act of fancy, she is transported to

a wild farm in Northumberland, well stocked with milk cows, yeald beasts, and sheep; a meeting house hard by, frequented by serious presbyterians, who had united in a harmonious call to Reuben Butler to be their spiritual guide; − Effie restored, not to gaiety, but to cheerfulness at least; − their father, with his grey hairs smoothed down, and spectacles on his nose; − herself with the maiden's snood exchanged for a matron's curch − all arranged in a pew in the said meeting house, listening to words of devotion, rendered sweeter and more powerful by the affectionate ties which combined them with the preacher.   (ch. 39; 237−38)

Jeanie's Northumbrian daydream is enacted, with some important modifications, on the Duke of Argyle's estate. The scenes at Roseneath express this fantasy with a patriotic turn, shifting the setting to the southwest Highlands. What Scott seeks to create in the Knocktarlitie episodes is an image of Scotland as an agrarian nation guided by the firm but temperate Presbyterianism of its clergy and ruled by the benevolent aristocracy embodied in the figure of Argyle.

The pastoral serves in *Midlothian* not only as an image of the good life and as a critical fiction against which the status quo is to be measured, but as a fiction of resolution. Knocktarlitie is a deliberately crafted response to the social problems described in the opening chapters. Like the reassuring conclusion of *Waverley*, the Roseneath scenes were written to create an artificial world in which history has lost its sting.[2] In Scott's imagined world, the Deanses and Butlers, having survived the trials of familial disorder, can begin their lives over again, without sacrificing the modest economic progress they had achieved in the years at St. Leonard's. Living within the enlarged circle of Jeanie's family, Davie can forget the sorrow and humiliation of Effie's seduction, and labor productively for a progressive landlord. In the improved Arcadia of Argyle's estate, virtuous labor is rewarded with material well-being. Davie gets a dairy-farm, Reuben is bestowed with a parish, and Jeanie presides over the household of a thriving family. The patterns of familial discontinuity established in the blighted affair of Effie and Staunton are, at least partially, reversed here.

The protruding pastoral in the last eight chapters of the novel is a result not merely of the author's greed or lack of taste, but of Scott's effort to compose in *Midlothian* a romance of national regeneration. Scott sets against one another two opposed versions of history and then attempts through the artifice of the Knocktarlitie episodes to reconcile those visions by subsuming the world of British politics within a unified and ahistorical vision. We find in the early chapters a richly detailed presentation of the events surrounding the execution of Captain Porteous, of the arrest of the smuggler Wilson and his cohort and the resentment of the Edinburgh mob at the brutal handling of Wilson's hanging. This is Scott the realist, mainly preoccupied with describing the tense relationship between the government and the mob, tracing in the gestures of the mob and the attitudes of his urban characters the shaping power of social and political forces on human actions, documenting the suffering brought about by the strife between nations. Scott gives in these opening chapters a convincing picture of a morally and politically decadent Britain, emphasizing this decadence through the sinister pattern of pardons which links the plight of Effie Deans with the killing of Porteous. Against this compelling account of a corrupt and oppressive society, Scott attempts to write a narrative of redemption, a story which centers on Jeanie Deans's "pilgrimage" to London and culminates in the pastoral fantasy of Knocktarlitie. In this counter-narrative, Scott leads a cow-feeder's daughter through an extended series of ordeals and shows her confronting and overcoming the obstructions in her path through an unshakeable, and socially determined, sense of right.

With her simple eloquence, Jeanie Deans becomes the voice of the true Scotland, speaking from the grassroots locus of the peasantry. The virtuous peasant stock which has produced Jeanie is one of the primary sources from which Scott believes the regeneration of Scotland, and, by implication, the Kingdom as a whole, must come. *Midlothian* thus reveals another facet of Scott's larger ideological position. *Waverley* and *The Bride of Lammermoor* discover a mind deeply preoccupied with the destruction of traditional social orders, with the decline of the ancient feudal aristocracy and the clan structure that had survived on the geographical peripheries of Britain. These works convey Scott's profound regret at the passing of the old ways and his desire for the restoration of a landed aristocracy which could somehow coexist harmoniously with the contemporary order. The political fantasy of a restored landed establishment is a significant pressure on the form of the novel.[3] In elevating Jeanie Deans to the position of a representative Scotswoman, Scott is emphasizing the virtues of a class which had hitherto been only a secondary subject in his fiction. At the opposite end of the novel's social hierarchy is the figure of Argyle. While Scott's celebration of the peasantry is genuine, Argyle cannot be neglected in any comprehensive discussion of the function of the pastoral in *Midlothian*. Argyle's social status as a progressive aristocrat, the scion of an old family who is skilled in the methods of modern power brokerage and a landlord knowledgeable in the latest techniques of agriculture, is a crucial element in the novel's character system. Having inserted Argyle as a benevolent intermediary in Jeanie's attempt to rescue her wayward sister, Scott withdraws his lordly helper to higher ground, setting the master at a distance from his servants at Knocktarlitie. In the Roseneath chapters, Argyle has become a horizon figure, absent from the daily activities of his estate, and yet a good landlord, bestowing the bounty of his wealth and property on a deserving tenantry.

The figure of Argyle represents the paternal authority which the Deanses and Butlers have lacked for so long, a landlord who is

generous toward his tenants and a political leader who is potent
and skillful in the arenas of Parliament and the court. The elder
Dumbiedikes is the first of their landlords, and the least fit to rule
the estate. While the younger Laird lacks his father's "grasping spirit
and active mind" (ch. 8; 122), he does little to improve the estate,
leaving much of his pasture land unenclosed, and raising a few crops
by the outmoded runrig method of his benighted predecessors. While
he does not actively oppress his tenants, he allows the crudely
appointed estate handed down to him by his father to fall into decay,
as Scott's description demonstrates in detail:

This inartificial edifice, exactly such as a child would build with cards, had
a steep roof flagged with coarse grey stones instead of slates ... One or two
dilapidated outhouses, connected by a courtyard wall equally ruinous,
surrounded the mansion. The court had been paved, but the flags being partly
displaced and partly renewed, a gallant crop of docks and thistles sprang up
between them, and the small garden, which opened by a postern through the
wall, seemed not to be in a much more orderly condition. Over the low arched
gateway which led into the yard, there was a carved stone, exhibiting some
attempt at armorial bearings; and above the inner entrance hung, and had
hung for many years, the mouldering hatchment, which announced that
umquhile Laurence Dumbie of Dumbiedikes, had been gathered to his fathers
in Newbattle kirkyard. The approach to this palace of pleasure was by a road
formed by the rude fragments of stone gathered from the fields, and it was
surrounded by ploughed but unenclosed land.   (ch. 26; 4–5)

Old Dumbiedikes had styled himself a country "gentleman," and
lived in accordance with a squire's standards of gentility. The " 'auld
laird,' " unlike his son, "wore a sword, kept a good horse, and a brace
of greyhounds; brawled, swore, and betted at cockfights and horse-
matches; followed Somerville of Drum's hawks, and the Lord Ross's
hounds ..." But the boisterous squire is succeeded by a passive
and retiring heir. The line, Scott remarks, "had been vailed of its
splendour in the present proprietor, who cared for no rustic amuse-
ments, and was as saving, timid, and retired as his father was grasping
and selfishly extravagant – daring, wild, intrusive" (ch. 26; 3). Scott's
satirical portrait of Old Dumbiedikes on his deathbed, of "Mammon
struggling with Remorse" (ch. 8; 121), is succeeded by a depiction of
an heir whose worst defects are a hoarding nature and an extraordinary lassitude in maintaining and improving his estate. The view
of the mansion and its environs argues "neglect and discomfort."

Its present condition is the product not of poverty, but of "mere idleness and indifference" (ch. 26; 5).

Contrasting with the degeneracy of the Dumbiedikes line is the improving spirit and agricultural skill of Argyle, who has set up an experimental farm at Knocktarlitie of which Davie Deans will be superintendent. On their return from the audience with the Queen, the Duke converses ably with Jeanie on the topics of husbandry and dairy-farming:

The Duke, besides his other patriotic qualities, was a distinguished agriculturalist, and proud of his knowledge in that department. He entertained Jeanie with his observations on the different breeds of cattle in Scotland, and their capacity for the dairy ...   (ch. 38; 217)

The stature of the Duke as a politician of extraordinary integrity, acting solely out of patriotic pride and solicitude for his fellow Scots, is established in the brief biographical sketch which precedes his first meeting with Jeanie Deans. Argyle is rendered here as at once a helping figure from the realm of folk-tale and a "real" Scottish politician, a historical figure with the power and generosity of a fairy-tale nobleman. The Duke of Argyle is a "benevolent enchanter" (ch. 43; 280), a powerful magician, who with a few flicks of his wand helps Jeanie to secure a royal pardon for her sister, bestows a parish upon Reuben Butler, and gives Davie his own dairy-farm.

While Argyle is, as Scott slyly notes, a "story-book" Duke (ch. 39; 229), he is also the embodiment of the enlightened aristocracy Scott saw as the right ruling authority of the nation. Scott's ideal society in *Midlothian* is a prosperous agrarian order which has as its base a close-knit family of peasant stock, protected and guided by an old and venerated Scottish family. Knocktarlitie can best be described as an improver's pastoral. The animals who graze in the green vales of Roseneath are bred and shepherded according to the very latest methods. In introducing the Deanses and Butlers, Scott shows them in an essentially feudal relationship with the Laird of Dumbiedikes, occupying small crofts on an estate which had fallen into decay with the general decline of feudal power in the region. With the death of the "auld laird," and under the benign neglect of his son, the families become interdependent, establishing a neighborly routine of practical aid and visitation. United by the common dangers of poverty and the daily rigors of cultivating the thin soil, the families grow close.

Relations between Jeanie Deans and Reuben Butler early become "strict and intimate." The future pillars of Knocktarlitie society are brought together as children in the routine tasks of farming, herding a handful of sheep and a few cows on the unenclosed common of Dumbiedikes's estate, playing together, attending school (ch. 9; 126–28). The self-contained agrarian world of the estate produces the plain-spoken and honest Jeanie, the novel's peasant heroine.

While existence on the estate is a struggle against poverty, the world outside offers little prospect for prosperity. Reuben Butler's early career is a short study in the limits of social mobility. Butler's education in divinity represents an opportunity for him to rise above his underclass origins. But when he leaves the small agricultural community in which he was raised to seek a better living, he encounters the obstacles of a rigid class structure. Denied a post as a schoolmaster at Dumfries because the son of a local laird is preferred over him, Butler is forced to accept a pathetic salary as an assistant schoolmaster in a small village near Edinburgh.

As time passes, the feudal relationship of laird and tenant lapses. Too infirm to handle the affairs of Beersheba, Mrs. Butler is forced to give the farm back to Dumbiedikes and live on as a mere resident of the house. After the death of his second wife, Davie Deans departs from Woodend and takes a situation as a cow-feeder at St. Leonard's Crag, abandoning the little farm which he had struggled so long to keep. In the vicissitudes experienced by the families, Scott depicts the decline of the small farm and intimate peasant community which engendered the novel's heroine, the gradual dissolution of the feudal ties which had bound the families to the land and to the landlord. In geographical terms, the move to St. Leonard's is also a move toward the city. But while the farm at St. Leonard's lies only half a mile from the outermost parts of the city, the two social worlds implied in the novel's geography remain isolated from one another in the early chapters. Mrs. Saddletree, the shopkeeper's wife, is a link between the rural world of St. Leonard's and the urban world of Edinburgh. But the event that ties the cow-feeder's family at St. Leonard's to the city is the seduction of Effie. Effie's departure from the farm continues the process of decline which began with the death of Rebecca Deans and the move to St. Leonard's, the series of events which will cause a violent rupture in the tightly woven fabric of the Deans family – a break which will prove irreparable.

Yet Effie's seduction and trial have at the same time an expansive and unifying force, serving to break down not only the structure of the family, but the cultural and social barriers between the pastoral realm of peasant life which the Deanses inhabit and the city life of Edinburgh and London. The impending trial of her sister brings the cow-feeder's daughter into the Edinburgh tolbooth, the very "Heart of Midlothian," forcing her into contact with the legal hierarchy of the city, and placing her face to face with the marginal figure of Ratcliffe, with his shadowy underworld connections. Effie's seduction draws Jeanie to the political centers of the Kingdom, and it is this exposure which allows Scott to claim for his heroine the representative value required for the novel's ideological ends. In order to make of Jeanie Deans an adequate redemptive figure, Scott must first bring her out of her rural enclave and into the heart of the city. If the cow-feeder's daughter is to save the nation, her journey must encompass the whole geographical and social entity. Scott's reversal of the *Waverley* pattern in bringing his heroine from Scotland to England extends the force of Jeanie's pilgrimage to the heart of Britain itself.[4] The journey is a key structural element of Scott's belated protest on behalf of his homeland against English cultural imperialism, a cautious and deferential form of national self-assertion. The range of Jeanie's experience on the road is designed to include every reach in the social hierarchy. Scott's broad social and geographical sweep represents an effort to assimilate within a single, unified spatial and temporal form the political and social disjunctions so sharply defined in the early chapters on the Porteous riots. As an ideological device, the journey serves a cohesive purpose, investing a humble underclass figure with the emblematic quality of a typical Scotswoman.

The journey brings Jeanie Deans into the company of coachmen, drivers, innkeepers, shopkeepers, peasants – people from the lower levels of the social order, to which she herself belongs. Waylaid by highwaymen near Grantham, Jeanie is kidnapped and held prisoner, with the madwoman Madge Wildfire as her guard (chapters 29–30). The assault of the highwaymen brings Jeanie into the novel's underworld, a realm with which she has hitherto had her only contact in the Edinburgh tolbooth. Willingham, the English village where Jeanie escapes from her captors, appears as a social oasis for the embattled pilgrim and a prevision of the scene which awaits her at the end of her journey. To Jeanie, the village seems one of those beautiful scenes which are so often found in merry England, where the cottages, instead of being built in two direct lines on each side of a dusty high road, stand in detached groups, interspersed not only with large oaks and elms, but with fruit trees, so many of which were at this time in flourish, that the grove seemed enammeled with their crimson and white blossoms. In the centre of the hamlet stood the parish church and its little Gothic tower, from which at present was heard the Sunday chime of bells.

(ch. 31; 96–97)

In this rural English idyll, Jeanie emerges from the perilous world of the criminal underclass and crosses yet another class boundary, entering the world of the English gentry in the rectory at Willingham. The relationship depicted in the scenes at Willingham between the elder and the younger Staunton represents one of the key social disjunctions of the novel. It is part of the pattern of familial discontinuity which Jeanie's pilgrimage is designed to heal. The elder Staunton is a veritable pillar of society, a clergyman, a magistrate, and the scion of an old landed family. His son is a fallen aristocrat, who, having descended into "low society," has, momentarily, resumed his proper identity. In the novel's scheme of class relations, Staunton/Robertson functions as a borderline figure by virtue of his mixed class affiliations, a figure belonging at once to two disparate worlds, and yet to neither. Staunton/Robertson combines the extremes of the social hierarchy. Aristocrat and mob leader, lord and smuggler, he is not only a link between the underworld and the upper class, but an allegorical character through which Scott makes a statement about the condition of the aristocracy. The relationship of father and son epitomizes the generational discontinuity and the absence of a stable ruling authority which Scott sees infecting the nation.

The inclusion of Willingham in Jeanie's journey works as a preliminary transition, providing a bridge from the lower to the higher reaches of society. Jeanie's emergence from the underworld is followed by a meteoric ascent to the topmost place in the social hierarchy. Her rise to the top stands in inverse parallel to Staunton/Robertson's descent into the depths of the criminal underworld. In pleading her sister's case, Jeanie, like Staunton, violates the social code of conduct for her class, daring to seek justice and mercy from her superiors. But while Staunton's violation proves destructive in its effect, Jeanie's is ameliorative. Her action serves at once to correct an injustice committed by the legal and political establishment and to ratify the status quo by eliciting its latent benevolence.

Jeanie's speech to the Queen completes a process of ethical transformation which began with her departure from the pastoral world of St. Leonard's.[5] The immediate force of Jeanie's language lies in its appeal to the Queen's presumed sense of mercy and spiritual anxiety concerning heavenly reward and punishment:

Alas! it is not when we sleep soft and wake merrily ourselves, that we think on other people's sufferings. Our hearts are waxed light within us then and we are for righting our ain wrongs and fighting our ain battles. But when the hour of trouble comes to the mind or to the body − and seldom may it visit your Leddyship − and when the hour of death comes, that comes to high and low − lang and late may it be yours − O, my Leddy, then it isna what we hae dune for oursells, but what we hae dune for others that we think on maist pleasantly. And the thoughts that ye hae intervened to spare the puir thing's life will be sweeter in that hour, come when it may, than if the word of your mouth could hang the haill Porteous mob at the tail of ae tow.
(ch. 37; 210)

The mixture of English with Scott's version of Lowland dialect creates a blunt and peculiarly "Scottish" style for the heroine. In *Midlothian*, virtue speaks the language of a Lowland peasant. That language, we must not fail to note, is a heavily anglicized vernacular, which gains currency and respectability by virtue of its English elements. Scott's peasant heroine preaches, for the benefit of her rulers, an ethic of justice and mercy against the harsh and oppressive ethic of English justice that has condemned Effie and subjected the citizens of Edinburgh to the burdens of official investigations and heavy fines. By directly linking Jeanie's pleas for her sister's life with the actions of the Porteous mob, Scott claims for his heroine a range of influence which takes in the whole political establishment of Britain.

The seemingly artless eloquence that works so well on the Queen becomes a positive aesthetic standard, the style in which truth and virtue must be rendered. Jeanie's "plain" style is implicitly contrasted with the "frantic style" of Staunton's speech and letters. Staunton's language is grandiloquent and sensational, spoken in a tone always verging on desperation, laden with appeals to the emotions and with claims of passionate concern for his victims. Just before Effie's trial, Staunton writes to Jeanie a letter which is at once imprecatory and imperious, begging and demanding that she meet him at Muschat's Cairn:

> If she would save a human being from the most damning guilt, and all its desperate consequences, − if she desired the life and honour of her sister to be saved from the bloody fangs of an unjust law, − if she desired not to forfeit peace of mind here and happiness hereafter ... she was entreated to give a sure, secret, and solitary meeting to the writer. She alone could rescue him ... and he only could rescue her.   (ch. 14; 229)

Convalescing after a riding accident suffered on his way to London to clear Effie's name, Staunton represents himself to Jeanie as "lying like a crushed snake, writhing with impotence at my incapacity of motion" (ch. 33; 126). The "frantic" style rejected by Scott is both a literary technique and the expressive vehicle of ethical and political attitudes which the novel rejects. Despite his claims of solicitude for his victim, Staunton's language suggests an obsession with the self's sensations and emotions that debases or excludes simple moral imperatives.

The Queen's simple and solemn compliment to Jeanie's address elevates the style of the cow-feeder's daughter to a place of primacy within the novel. Against Jeanie's eloquence, Staunton's vehement expressions of guilt and compassion ring false. His violent posturings in the meeting at Muschat's Cairn epitomize Staunton's style. His language is a series of hollow gestures, theatrical poses assumed as a way of eliciting sympathy or of threatening his hearer into complicity. In contrast, Jeanie's inability to dissimulate, to use language as a means of deception for any reason, is meant to appear as a positive virtue. Following her audience with the Queen, Jeanie performs the unaccustomed act of letter-writing. In a disarmingly blunt opening sentence, she declares in a brief letter to her sister's seducer her purpose in writing: "To prevent farder mischieves, whereof there hath been enough, comes these ..." In the narrowest sense, the purpose of Jeanie's letter is to prevent any recurrence of disorder within her own family, and to restore the pattern of relationship which was violated in Effie's seduction. Jeanie's letter places Staunton's actions within a moral and religious perspective, re-asserting in the same gesture the unity of the Deans family, which was ruptured by Staunton, and the divine order from which Staunton remains an outcast: "So sir, I pray for your better welfare in body and soul, and that it will please the fisycian to visit you in his good time. Alwaies, sir, I pray you will never come to see my sister, whereof there has been too much" (ch. 39; 224). With Effie now pardoned, Jeanie prays that her sister's profligate lover will be saved from his sins. But her prayer for redemption is also a gesture of exclusion, in which the sinner's salvation is linked with an end to his relationship with her sister.

The power of Jeanie's eloquence is extended in her letters to her father and fiancé, as if the blunt force of her language could not only heal the deep wounds within her family, but also remove the social divisions within the Kingdom. The letter to her father announces Effie's pardon straightaway, then presents Caroline as a figure on a par with "other grand leddies" − not as a powerful and mysterious force, but as a recognizable social type. While there is more than a trace of peasant superstition and awe in Jeanie's description of the Queen, the tendency of her language is to reduce the figure of the monarch to a comprehensible person with extraordinary traits:

And I spoke with the Queen face to face, and yet live; for she is not muckle differing from other grand leddies, saving that she has a stately presence, and een like a blue huntin' hawk's ...

Jeanie presents Argyle in the letter as the primary agent of "all this good." Yet he is not, for her, a "benevolent enchanter," but rather "a native and true-hearted Scotsman." She praises the Duke not only for his timely aid, but for his surprising modesty and his keen grasp of animal husbandry: "not pridefu', like other folk we ken of − and likewise skeely enow in bestial" (ch. 39; 225).

Through Jeanie Deans, then, the novel gives expression to an ideal of simple and unadulterated peasant virtue, and places the intricate and sinister world of the English court within its purview. Jeanie's innocence is impervious to the jealousies which shape the Queen's attitude toward her Scottish subjects, and this incapacity to see things from the perspective of the court enhances the power of her address. In the audience with Caroline, plain virtue overwhelms courtly sophistication. Jeanie's unreflecting commitment to speaking the truth allows her to survive her inadvertent errors of diplomacy and finally to carry her plea.

The moral theme of the nature of truth is based in the novel on two opposing ideas of the relationship between language and reality.

At Effie's trial, Jeanie can only tell the magistrates that her sister had said nothing to her about her pregnancy. She cannot speak an untruth, even to save her sister's life. The simple deception suggested by Staunton and later by Effie's lawyers might have prevented a conviction. But Jeanie refuses to use language to conceal the truth as she knows it. Van Ghent's misplaced emphasis on the novel's under-developed moral vision has merely distracted attention from Scott's ambivalent relationship to his own fictions.[6] Jeanie's adherence to truth is grounded in a radically representational notion of how language ought to be used, based on the assumption that there can be a genuine correspondence between word and world, language and reality. In the courtroom, Jeanie will not declare that an event occurred that did not, in simple fact, take place. From her perspective, Staunton's desperate pleas that she dissemble in order to save her sister bespeak a moral degeneracy. But Staunton's entreaties, along with the advice of Effie's lawyers at the trial, imply that language is the vehicle of moral and political intentions, and not simply a medium for stating things as they are.

The audience with the Queen is the meeting point, then, of two styles and two conceptions of language. From the perspective of the Queen and the Duke, schooled in the ways of the court, Jeanie's language is not simply an expression of truth, but an instrument for saying one thing while intending another. To the Queen, Jeanie's naive defense of her country against the implication of barbarism is a subtle reminder of King George's dispute with the Prince of Wales. The explanation Jeanie offers for the common occurrence of child murder in Scotland is interpreted by Lady Suffolk as a rebuke for her adulterous relationship with the King. The scene could perhaps be read as a lesson in the power of reader reception and the force of context in shaping the meaning of a speech act. But the dominant force in the meeting is finally sincerity, which is epitomized in Jeanie's heartfelt appeal for clemency.

Scott's conservatism in *Midlothian* is thus linked through the figure of Jeanie Deans with a conception of language which approaches the Adamic. The voice of Jeanie Deans is the voice of unreflecting virtue, emanating directly from the heart, against the corrupt language of a degenerate society. In the degraded world of the court, language is an instrument of policy, a vehicle of narrowly political ends, a weapon which may be used without regard to its truth content.

Words always have a double meaning, an allegorical or metaphorical value which exceeds the bounds of simple denotation – the limits within which Scott's literal-minded heroine thinks and speaks. The Queen wonders at the beginning of the meeting if Jeanie is a rude country paramour of the Duke or a poor relation whom he is presenting in the hope of gaining some favor for her. But Jeanie, oblivious to the contextual significance of her dress and speech, presents herself to the Queen without the mask of a self-conscious style. Her authenticity wins the day. Jeanie means exactly what she says, and the essential integrity of her words and their meaning conquer even the Queen.

With her unqualified commitment to linguistic precision, Jeanie is the embodiment of anti-fiction.[7] Yet despite his valorization of Jeanie's sincerity, Scott remains committed to fabulation. Scott wrote *Midlothian* not merely as a faithful depiction of a crisis in British history, but as a story about the past, an interpretation of a great historical moment that culminates in an elaborate projection of a better Scotland. *Midlothian* was written with a particular political intention, as a means of placing historical reality at a comfortable distance. The primary motive of Scott's art is to rewrite history in such a way as to accommodate all the levels of the social hierarchy, to resolve the tensions within Scotland and to reconcile Scotland and England within the received form of the Union. Once the novel is understood as a romance of regeneration, its formal disjunctions can be grasped as seams in the fabric, flaws produced in the effort to exclude history from the lines of the novel.

The aesthetic problems with the novel have been discussed too thoroughly and too often to need much reiteration here.[8] To merely complain about the disparity between the Knocktarlitie scenes and the Edinburgh chapters or the intrusion of inferior genres into what could have been a great moral and psychological study seems to me futile. The Knocktarlitie episodes must be understood as part of a serious response to real social and political contradictions. In assuming the novel's incoherence and in dwelling too long over the author's presumed confusion, we may ignore Scott's attempt to create a world in language which will displace the world which he perceives as corrupt, to transcend by fictive means the very conditions which the novel itself describes. To claim the historical veracity of the Knocktarlitie scenes, as a repentant Thomas Crawford does in revising his study of the novel, is simply to err in another direction.[9] The issue is not the relative truth content of the novel, but the way in which the novel's formal patterns disguise and betray the conflicts which they are intended to conceal.

To grasp the relationship between the disparate social worlds of the novel, we must see the journey of Jeanie Deans, in formal terms, as an effort to repudiate the decadence depicted in the early chapters and to reform the corrupt order which pardoned Porteous and condemned Effie. The narrative begins in the vein of Scott's vaunted realism,[10] with the depiction of an urban world in which violent crime is sanctioned, tacitly and overtly, by the governing authorities, and justice is meted out not by the legal guardians of order, but by the actions of the mob. Truth has no language in this world, no place in its political and legal system. Jeanie must either tell a lie or see her sister go to the gallows for a crime which may never have been committed. Beyond the general corruption in government, there is the more immediate threat to the integrity of the family. The novel is marked among Scott's works for the persistence with which it exploits and seeks to eliminate patterns of discontinuity within the structure of the family. With the crucial exception of Jeanie's unswerving loyalty to her father and sister, the family situations in the novel suggest a widespread social decline.

Effie's seduction makes her an outcast in the eyes of her father. Before the trial, Davie Deans disavows her (ch. 18; 312), and with her decision to join Staunton after her pardon, she becomes to him "a withered branch [which] will never bear fruit of grace – a scapegoat gone forth into the wilderness of the world, to carry wi' her, as I trust, the sins of our little congregation" (ch. 42; 273). But Effie's seduction is not only a violation of Davie's moral and religious laws. It is a transgression of class-determined rules of behavior. Within the moral and social perimeters tacitly asserted in the novel, the real crime committed by Effie and Staunton, the sin for which they are punished, is not merely adultery, but the violation of unwritten rules against the intermingling of peasant and aristocrat. The elaborate devices of masking which Effie uses in her role as Staunton's wife, the cultivation of superior manners, the acquisition of foreign languages, the refinements of spelling and penmanship, serve not simply to conceal her sexual act, but to disguise her class origins, her social identity as the second daughter of a Lowland peasant.

The cultural malaise of familial discontinuity reflects the political disequilibrium of Scotland's relationship with England. Scott's method of presentation invites us to read the novel as a piece of political allegory. *Midlothian* represents an ambitious – and ultimately unsuccessful – attempt to link together the political, the cultural, and the moral realms, to show how a great political crisis is reflected, and, in turn, altered, by events within the circle of the family, and within the individual conscience. In the disordered world rendered in the Edinburgh chapters, the personal fortitude of Jeanie Deans would be of little avail without the sanction of monarchical power. What is expressed in Scott's treatment of British politics is not, however, a royalist nostalgia for the monarchical authority of past ages,[11] but the longing of a bourgeois Tory for a moderate and merciful ruling authority in place of a government perceived as corrupt and oppressive.

The restorative force of Jeanie's gesture takes in the socio-political order at all its levels. The journey to London is a mission of reconciliation, aimed at revitalizing both the Deans family and the greater family of Britain. As an ideological action, Jeanie's journey is basically conservative in thrust. Her request for a pardon is not a radical cry for justice on behalf of the lower classes, but a salutary reminder to the established order of its own better judgment. The motive of Jeanie's triumphant career is to ratify the socio-political hierarchy which Scott believed was the present and future hope of the nation. Jeanie Deans departs from her lowly station to plead her sister's case with her country's rulers, counting on their compassion and relying on their power. In arguing for mercy, Jeanie is at once violating and reinforcing the given order of the Kingdom. She is a reactionary rebel, whose momentary disruption of the status quo serves to evoke from its highest authorities the justice and mercy of which they are capable. What is restored in these pastoral scenes is the proper relation between ruler and subject, an order in which the ruler is a sustaining and protective force.

Jeanie's audience with the Queen is a means of bringing the wayward Effie back within the charmed circle envisioned at the outset of the journey. At the close of the novel, we are told that Jeanie and Reuben, "happy in each other, in the prosperity of their family, and the love and honour of all who knew them ... lived beloved and died lamented" (ch. 52; 446). Yet the happiness of Jeanie's family is limited to its immediate circle, and that circle does not include Effie. Effie's commitment to Staunton has taken her beyond the redemptive force of filial affection, beyond the power of Jeanie's healing word. In returning to her seducer, Effie places herself outside the emotional and social valence of the Deanses and the Butlers, rejecting the moral authority of her sister and father to follow the dictates of her own passion. In Effie's career, the individual will and the related force of sexual desire take predominance over the bonds of family.

Their adherence to the laws of passion isolates Effie and Staunton from Jeanie's world, from the benign and stable social order asserted in the Roseneath episodes. Staunton serves as a Gothic straw man for Scott, evoking not only the literature whose forms of expression Scott has rejected, but an ideological amalgam which can have no place in the novel's ideal society. In writing Effie and Staunton into banishment, the novel rejects the hierarchy of value implicit in their affair, the primacy of individual fulfillment, of sheer passional attachment and erotic feeling over filial affection and communal harmony. Happiness in *Midlothian* is finally the property of the virtuous, and virtue excludes the turbulent emotions which have brought Effie and Staunton together. Jeanie Deans and Reuben Butler are happy and prosperous. Their remarkably durable engagement was made of less volatile stuff: "Fortunately for the lovers, their passion was of no ardent or enthusiastic cast; and a sense of duty on both sides induced them to bear, with patient fortitude, the protracted interval which divided them from each other" (ch. 9; 140). The moderate quality of their "passion" is an essential condition of its long survival through years of hardship and separation. While the more violent emotions of Effie and Staunton might well have appealed to the genteel tastes of Scott's readership, Knocktarlitie is not their world. They are romantic foils, introduced as the agents of values which the novel criticizes and finally negates.[12] The Effie/Staunton plot works as a counter-narrative to the central action and as a challenge to the political and social beliefs which Scott seeks to endorse in *Midlothian*. But while its melodramatic scenes detract from the force of Scott's pastoral, it remains throughout a subservient narrative, an instrument of Scott's political intentions. The novel's romantic hero and heroine serve finally as examples of what will become of those who ignore the beneficent constraints of familial and public order, and give themselves over to desire. In these unhappy lovers, the novel evokes figures of disruptive desire in order to purge the anarchic forces they embody from its fictive social world, to protect the order of which Jeanie Deans is a mainstay.

Scott's tendency to exploit anti-realistic genres in the service of a conservative political vision persists in *Midlothian* in several forms, of which the Gothic/romantic counterplot of Effie and her dark seducer is only the most prominent instance. Scott's disposition to literary trickery is given a new twist in *Midlothian*.[13] In Edward Waverley, Scott had drawn a fanciful hero, a figure given to imaginative excess. Waverley wanders into the Highlands out of sheer romantic curiosity, and is carried out of the land of romance by the vicissitudes of civil war. Having shed his defects of vision, he returns to Scotland, where, in one of Scott's most flagrantly fanciful endings, he restores a decayed feudal estate, marries the daughter of its proprietor, and presumably lives on to enjoy his elevated social position and his superabundance of property. In *Midlothian*, a romantic imagination is no longer simply a remediable weakness of vision, but a flaw which is both self-destructive and dangerous to the integrity of the family and the nation. Scott works a change in Edward Waverley, an alteration in his hero's perspective on the past which allows him to set Waverley on the winning side in the civil war. But in *Midlothian*, figures of imagination are ultimately relegated to banishment and death. Staunton is not reformed by Scott, but cast out of the novel's romance of regeneration.

In *Waverley* or *The Bride*, the Gothic/Byronic Staunton might have done service as a belated chivalric hero, trapped within the obsolescent consciousness of a moribund social order, acting in accordance with a long-abandoned feudal ethos.[14] But in the harsher world of *Midlothian*, such heroism is not merely out of date, but a positive threat to public order. *Waverley* implies through the necessary death of Fergus MacIvor and the peaceful assimilation of the Baron of Bradwardine that Jacobite feudalism represents the last, glorious stand of the ancient order of Scotland. With its cheerful fiction of reconciliation, *Waverley* suggests that the feudal order has been supplanted by an enlightened and progressive aristocracy, and that the transition in political power and the corollary change in social relations, momentous as they are, have permitted the preservation of traditional ways and manners. With its shift in social subject to the lower orders and its Presbyterian peasant heroine, *Midlothian* implies a broadening of Scott's political sympathies.[15] The scenes at Roseneath reflect this change of subject. Much as the restored Tully-Veolan represents the assimilation of the old feudal establishment and the preservation of its central icons, Knocktarlitie serves as a social symbol of resolution. In contrast to the Baron's estate, Knocktarlitie is a vital agrarian society, of which the Butlers, now a lower-gentry family of peasant origin, are the primary cohesive force. But despite the apparent expansion of Scott's sympathies, the novel retains a rigorous principle of exclusion. Staunton is an outcast from the novel's central social world throughout. *Déclassé* at the outset, Staunton remains a marginal figure even after he resumes his original class identity.

Although Scott might have finished with Staunton in the Willingham scenes, he extends the career of his Gothic character to the novel's final chapter. Scott's persistent use of the figure is difficult to explain within the formal and thematic contours of the novel. If, as Van Ghent has suggested, the novel's best feature is its unfortunately attenuated study of Jeanie Deans's moral dilemma, then Staunton is merely a Gothic appendage. If we follow Robin Mayhead's cue and read *Midlothian* as an elaborate discourse on the great theme of Justice, then the tempestuous Staunton is an annoying distraction.[16] But simply to dismiss the whole Effie/Staunton plot as a botched job is not enough. Nor is it sufficient to suggest, as Shaw does, that Scott completed the melodramatic career of Staunton in the confidence that "his depiction of the prosaic Jeanie Deans has been so strong that we will prefer her heroism to the heroics of Staunton."[17]

Scott's extravagant subplot intrudes upon the pastoral world of Knocktarlitie as if it were an interpolation from another novel. The closing chapter of the novel is given largely to the completion of an action that appears to bear only an indirect relation to the happy conclusion of Jeanie Deans's sojourn. Yet while Scott's extension of the Effie/Staunton affair to the final pages of the novel may seem gratuitous, it allows him to complete an important thematic pattern. The epilogue to the novel sums up the organizing principle of the closing chapters:

This tale will not be told in vain if it shall be found to illustrate the great truth, that guilt, though it may attain temporal splendour, can never confer real happiness; that the evil consequences of our crimes long survive their commission, and like the ghosts of the murdered, forever haunt the steps of the malefactor; and that the paths of virtue, though seldom those of worldly greatness, are always those of pleasantness and peace. (ch. 52; 446)

These final didactic remarks emphasize moral issues. The lesson conveyed here is illustrated in the novel's closing judgment on the Butlers' life at Roseneath, the happy conclusion which caps off a rather hasty summary of Effie's blighted career: "Meanwhile, happy in each other, in the prosperity of their family, and the love and honour of all who knew them, this simple pair lived beloved and died lamented" (ch. 52; 446). After shipping Effie to a convent on the Continent to live out her life in seclusion, Scott returns us quickly to the charmed family circle of the Butlers for a rapid resolution to the novel's protracted action.

This extraordinarily short and sweet conclusion can be regarded as adequate only if we confine our attention to Scott's pictures of life in the pleasant valleys of Knocktarlitie. In the Knocktarlitie chapters, Scott has shifted the geopolitical center of Scotland away from the corrupt and conflict-ridden world of Edinburgh to a rural agrarian community. The novel's presentation of life in Roseneath is mainly concerned with preserving the elements of the old feudal order that were worth keeping and eliminating its vices. In place of the Lairds of Dumbiedikes, Scott gives us the enlightened and humane Argyle, an expert in agriculture, keenly interested in all matters pertaining to his land. The Duke's interest in husbandry and dairy-farming is a significant link between landlord and tenant, a bond which unites people of disparate status in a common pursuit. But Argyle still retains certain feudal prerogatives, using the privilege of patronage to bestow the Knocktarlitie ministry on Reuben Butler. Argyle's Roseneath is remarkable for its equilibrium, for the harmonious stasis of its social life. Butler ministers to an active parish of regular churchgoers, and with the aid of the Duke's bailiff, Duncan of Knockdunder, presides over a community relatively free of disruptive influences.

The political struggles depicted in the early chapters of the novel are largely absent from Knocktarlitie. But with the repeated references to the lawless Highlands, to the quiet presence of smugglers, and to the bandits in the hills, the threat of disruption persists. While Fleishman argues that these elements reflect the persistence of realistic motives,[18] Scott's robbers appear not as political criminals, but as fugitives from an inferior bandit romance. Donacha du na Dunaigh, it turns out, is not the product of a disenfranchised Highland clan who has turned to banditry as a means of survival and a gesture of defiance, but simply a local tinker who saw more profit in the disorder ensuing from the recent war than in his own trade. The figure of Duncan of Knockdunder could have been a serious historical portrait of Highlands mingled with Lowlands, half-bandit and half-baliff. Knockdunder's covert connections with the local criminal element could perhaps be read as a skillful rendering of the intimate ties between the agrarian community at Roseneath and the indigenous criminal element of the region. But Knockdunder is a piece of caricature, a rough-hewn clown most notable for his smoking, his excessive drinking, and his profuse swearing, a figure whose historical function as a sort of Scottish Mafioso is exceeded by his comic absurdity.

The Knocktarlitie episodes involve a far more effective strategy of evasion than the stylized depiction of underworld figures. The scenes on Roseneath occur during a fifteen-year span, a period that saw the last of the major Jacobite uprisings. Yet the civil war which had posed a serious threat to the stability of the London regime, and which led to the final subjugation of the Highlands, is alluded to only in passing. The English conquest of the Highlands, the military struggles waged in the region, and the ensuing social and cultural dislocations become a piece of backdrop to the novel's central action:

> After the breaking out and suppression of the rebellion in 1745, the peace of the country, adjacent to the Highlands, was considerably disturbed. Marauders, or men that had been driven to that desperate mode of life, quartered themselves in the fastnesses nearest to the Lowlands, which were the scene of their plunder ...   (ch. 49; 367)

Scott's attenuated and hazy account of the consequences of the 1745 rebellion transforms a crucial moment in the history of British colonialism into the distant cause of some relatively minor social disturbances. The strategy of distancing which is overtly thematized and repeatedly practiced in *Waverley* and *Old Mortality* is employed once again in this passage, most forcefully in the narrator's reminder to the reader of the relative stability of the present: "There is scarce a glen in the romantic and now peaceable Highlands of Perth, Stirling, and Dunbartonshire where one or more did not take up their residence" (ch. 49; 367). From the compositional present of the early nineteenth century, the "marauders" who ranged the back country of Argyleshire more than "sixty years since" appear as a now extinct source of disruption in a generally peaceful community.

The larger social organization of these chapters is a politicized version of Scott's brief epilogue, of that simple moral theme of virtue rewarded and wickedness punished asserted in the final lines of *Midlothian*. From Edward Waverley's elevation into property, we can see how Scott rewards with wealth and power those who find what he considers to be the right side in the historical struggle. *Midlothian* rehearses the pattern established in *Waverley*, but with significant changes in the status of both the winners and the losers. Reuben Butler's excursion to Edinburgh allows Scott to complete his scheme of reward and punishment. Once poor and downtrodden, eking out a subsistence wage as an assistant schoolmaster, deprived of an ample living by a system of preferment which favors the sons of the gentry, Butler is now a prominent member of the Scottish kirk. Butler's ascent to a secure position within the religious establishment is emphasized in the Edinburgh episode and contrasted to the situation of Staunton. Butler is now "generally respected by those of his own profession, as well as by the laity ... He had made several public appearances in the Assembly ... and he was followed and admired as a sound, and at the same time, as an eloquent preacher" (ch. 51; 410). With Staunton, the point of emphasis is the radical alteration in social costuming from past to present: "Walking at the right hand of the representative of Sovereignty, covered with lace and embroidery, and all the paraphernalia of wealth and rank ... Who could have recognized in a form so aristocratic the plebeian convict, that, disguised in the rags of Madge Wildfire, had led the formidable rioters in their destined revenge?" (ch. 51; 405).

This picture of Staunton walking in the Lord Commissioner's procession reiterates the duality of aristocrat and rebel which has marked Staunton throughout. Staunton has come to the city in search of his lost son. His obsessive search for his heir gives the closing chapter of the novel yet a further Gothic turn, a modal pattern reinforced in the scene of Staunton's murder. That Staunton should die at the hands of his own son, now a denizen of the underworld, shifts the concluding pages of the novel into a generic realm clearly incongruous with the pastoral pattern asserted on Jeanie's arrival at Knocktarlitie. Beneath this formal disjunction is one version of a violent political fantasy that recurs throughout the Waverley novels, a fantasy of subjugation directed at once toward the underclass and the aristocracy. In the figure of Staunton, the novel combines the dual threat of a degenerate aristocracy and a rebellious underclass. The ideological message of Staunton's chequered career is a mixture of fascination and revulsion, in which revulsion finally takes precedence. According to the "Epilogue," Staunton's violent death represents the just punishment of the wicked. It is, at the same time, a fitting penalty for Staunton's political crimes. Staunton's son, the "Whistler," is the offspring of a transgressive coupling, of illicit intercourse between a peasant and an aristocrat. At the geographical margin of Roseneath, Staunton encounters his son and heir, the pure product of his sins. The "Whistler" is a debased version of the plebeian convict who led the mob against Captain Porteous, an image of Staunton's plebeian self arising from the novel's underworld to destroy him.

The motive behind Staunton's career is to debunk an ideology that poses a threat to the form of social order in which Scott believes. In punishing Staunton and Effie, the novel accomplishes the exclusionary gesture which was denied the British government, killing off the leader of the Porteous riot and sending his paramour into banishment from family and homeland. The fate of this unhappy pair is intended to show that those who violate the laws of the state and the laws of God must pay dearly for their sins. While Effie and Staunton succeed in evading the force of the law, they cannot escape the pattern of fatality that seems to determine the form of Scott's historical romances.

On the winning side, Jeanie Deans, her mission of rescue accomplished, receives the just reward of virtue, a central place in Argyle's Arcadia. The Roseneath community in which Jeanie and Reuben "lived beloved and died lamented" is founded, on the one hand, upon a progressive and humane landed establishment, and on the other, an intelligent, hard-working and thrifty peasantry. But the vision that emerges in the later chapters of the novel is both regenerative and evasive in effect. It is at once an image of a healthy and prosperous nation and a means of concealing the very conflicts the novel itself has documented.

THE BRIDE OF LAMMERMOOR: HISTORY AS DREAMWORK

Knocktarlitie is a literary realm, a verbal world that serves, like the fairy-tale ending of *Waverley*, as an instrument of revision. In these final chapters, historical detail is appropriated to lend concreteness to an ahistorical fiction. History is reduced to a decorative function, employed as a stage property against which Scott's ideal of agrarian prosperity is defined and valorized. Scott's pastoral does, of course, contain elements that are "historical" in the narrowest sense. We know from Scott's 1830 "Introduction" to the novel that the pilgrimage of Jeanie Deans was based on the "real life" story of Helen Walker. We are aware that the Duke of Argyle played a significant role outside *The Heart of Midlothian*, as Scott observes, with a certain amount of patriotic exaggeration, in his short biographical sketch. And in the figures of Jeanie and David Deans, we find an earnest attempt at authentic historical portrayal, an effort sharply at odds with the main thrust of the Knocktarlitie episodes.

To suggest that Roseneath is an accurate depiction of life on Argyle's estate, that it is anything other than a picture of the past, is to be fooled by Scott's elaborate tricks. What is lacking in the early urban scenes of the novel, and what Scott attempts to create, is a middle ground between the novel's political extremes, between the unruly tenants of Scotland and their harsh and oppressive landlord. Scott seeks a position that is neither radically anti-Union nor obsequiously pro-British, that can somehow accommodate both sides of a conflict that has rocked the Scottish nation and disturbed the peace of the Kingdom. But the aesthetic failure of Scott's resolution serves instead to remind us of the social and political contradictions it was intended to disguise.

Scott attempted to present in the final chapters of *Midlothian* what he believed to be the basis of a regenerate nation. Composed during a period marked by violent class conflict in England and Scotland, the Knocktarlitie scenes constitute a symbol of reconciliation. The final chapters of the novel represent an effort to reunite the Scottish nation after a century of civil strife, to heal the deep rifts brought about by the movement of history. In *The Bride of Lammermoor* (1819), Scott's meditations on the consequences of the Union culminate in a deeply pessimistic vision of historical change. *The Bride* lacks not only a compensatory narrative, such as the fable of national regeneration which had its culmination in the Knocktarlitie pastoral, but any symbol in which the conflicts between classes and political parties can be resolved, or at least held in stable form. Even the familiar and comforting convention Scott had used so unabashedly in earlier novels, the social fiction of felicitous marriage, is absent here.

It would be convenient to point to a historical crisis that parallels the situation in the novel, and then to observe the ways in which Scott renders its essential elements.[19] But the central critical problem posed by *The Bride* is, as I see it, to establish the motives, at once aesthetic and political, that have generated the form of the novel, to understand why *The Bride* should appear to readers as an attempt to fuse together conflicting representational modes and how the novel's formal strategies work to resolve the very conflicts they express.[20] The typical pattern for Scott's lovers is to "inherit a superabundance of real property"[21] and to enjoy a happy and prosperous matrimonial union. Although Welsh's description of the novels' motives is less broadly applicable than he has claimed, it can be usefully extended to *The Bride* as a measure of the degree to which the novel repeats and deviates from the dominant pattern of the denouement. Taking off from Welsh's argument, we can say that one of the primary motives shaping the form of the novel is the imperative of restoring the rights of the dispossessed heir to the Ravenswood estate, of bestowing upon the scion of an ancient landed family his proper portion of power. Despite the editorial distance of the novel's narrative voice, the hero's lingering sensitivity to the claims of his family registers a deep anxiety about the decline of the feudal aristocracy and a longing for the revival of the feudal virtues lacking from the social relations of the new order. The duality of allegiance so clearly visible in the figure of Ravenswood pervades *The Bride* at every level of its structure. Practically from the beginning of the novel, Ravenswood is presented as a dispossessed heir within two distinct, yet closely related, plots. Behind the Dalrymple legend related in the "Author's Introduction," we can see at work a narrative of the decline and fall of an ancient aristocratic family and the appropriation of its property by an upstart bourgeois antagonist, the same basic material worked in the earlier *Guy Mannering* (1815).

In dating the family's decline by its coincidence with the fall and exile of James II (and VII) and in suggesting that the late Lord

Ravenswood's espousal of the Stuart cause precipitated the fall, the novel provides a comprehensive historical explanation of Edgar Ravenswood's degraded condition. Intertwined with this historical plot are fragments of plots from the literary world of Gothic romance, in which a dispossessed heir proclaims a curse against the usurpers of his patrimonial rights and swears to avenge his family's loss of honor and fortune, then lays aside his mission of revenge to seek the hand of a woman, his enemy's beautiful daughter. The modal mixture visible in this combination of plots is a result of the novel's reworking of the political fantasies at its core.[22] David Punter has recently reminded us of the ways in which Gothic fiction embodied in disguised form the political and sexual obsessions of the newly dominant middle class.[23] Punter describes eighteenth-century Gothic as an expression of the thwarted desires of bourgeois culture in the trappings of a stylized feudal aristocracy. With the sense of historical distance created by this costuming, Gothic fiction permitted the expression of unconscious wishes without threatening the stability of public life. The attitude of Gothic toward the past was a "compound of repulsion and attraction," an ambivalent mixture in which fear of the aristocracy, of its violence and of the threat which it posed to the present, is combined with a longing for the past.[24] The historical thrust of Gothic is always dual. In giving form to bourgeois political fantasies, Gothic serves at once as a means of expressing anxieties about old class enemies and of transcoding the violence of the contemporary social order. The formal procedures of Gothic are an attempt to produce the historical present as a mysterious past and to reduce the threat of the past by rendering it in the familiar terms of contemporary reality.

While the apparently compassionate rationalism of *The Bride*'s narrating voice encourages sympathy towards the feudal protagonist, the tone of that voice is distinctly patronizing, as a glance at the novel's opening scene will show. The house to which Ravenswood returns after his father's funeral is a crumbling castle lying near the margin of what was once the Ravenswoods' extensive demesne. Gothic in mode, the castle serves as an outward sign of its master's spiritual condition at this moment. What we see here is the exploitation of Gothic machinery in a passage designed to demonstrate the subjective and irrational grounds of Ravenswood's perceptions. Scott turns the tables here, using a Gothic symbol in the process of demystifying

Gothic consciousness. In the narrator's analysis of Ravenswood's psychological condition, "the tarnished honour and degraded fortunes of his house, the destruction of his own hopes, and the triumph of that family by whom they had been ruined," are rendered as figments of Ravenswood's imagination, mere "phantoms" created by a mind "naturally of a gloomy cast." The question that closes the scene and the chapter reveals one of the novel's fundamental patterns for assimilating and neutralizing the supernatural force alluded to in the peasant's account of the "fatal night": "Alas! What fiend can suggest more dangerous counsels, than those adopted under the guidance of our own violent and unresisted passions?" (ch. 2; 38)[25] The narrator's language instructs the reader to regard Ravenswood as the unfortunate victim of his own untrammeled emotions. The implication is that we, narrator and reader, are superior to Ravenswood because we know that his gestures are the result of a lack of control. From our vantage point outside of Ravenswood's Gothic enclave, it appears that his rebellious fervor springs not from a rationally grounded sense of his family's victimization, but from the workings of an isolated and misguided mind. In league with the novel's narrating voice, we translate the mysterious forces embodied in the feudal figure of Ravenswood into the intelligible terms of human psychology.

By the insinuation that the threat of rebellion is merely the product of a doomed aristocrat's febrile imagination, the novel reduces to manageable form the "evil fiend" (ch. 2; 38) which it has itself evoked. In *The Bride*, the threat to social order is located in an atrophying aristocracy, a class which is, by virtue of its very condition, incapable of bringing its threats to fruition. Malise Ravenswood's revenge finally remains an element of local tradition, a story of usurpation and revenge often recalled but never repeated. Scott placed the legend near the beginning of the novel as a generic standard of measure, an element which will not only show the distance between Edgar Ravenswood and his ancestor, but also between Ravenswood and the hero of Gothic romance. Between Malise and Edgar, the novel tells us, the revolutions of English and Scottish history have intervened, and the surviving heir of the line is now Lord Ravenswood by courtesy only. Sir William Ashton is not a version of Walpole's Manfred, but merely a middle-class parvenu whose family fortunes have risen just as the fortunes of the Ravenswoods have declined.

But our attention in the early chapters is absorbed less by the issues of Scottish politics sketched there than by the legendary elements woven into the novel's historical plot. As he composes an account of the elder Lord Ravenswood's funeral which will show Edgar Ravenswood to be the instigator of a serious public disturbance, the Lord Keeper glances by chance at the Ravenswood family crest carved in the ceiling of his library. He sees a "black bull's head, with the legend, 'I bide my time'" (ch. 3; 42), and the story of Malise Ravenswood's revenge mingles itself with his reflections. According to local tradition, the rightful proprietor of the Ravenswood estate, deprived of his lands by a powerful usurper, returns to the castle in the guise of a tradesman, and with the help of a few faithful retainers, puts to death the usurper and his followers. The placing of a bull's head, an "ancient symbol of death," on the usurper's banquet table served as a signal for the enactment of the counterplot. After recounting the story to himself, the Lord Keeper sets aside his letter to the Privy Council and considers the consequences of sending an incriminating report.

While Scott never actually suggests that Ashton believes the legend to be true or expects it to be repeated, the story of Malise's revenge has a charge for Ashton which cannot be explained away simply by pointing to Scott's demystifications of the Gothic. Ashton's moment of hesitation contains a brief fluttering of the anxiety which motivates the novel's use of Gothic elements. In Ashton's reflections, a relatively minor violation of Scottish law is linked with the revenge of Malise Ravenswood: the manageable threat of the present is linked with a lethal threat from a legendary past. What disturbs the Lord Keeper and leads him to reconsider the step he is about to take is not the actual personage of Edgar Ravenswood, but the legendary figure of Ravenswood's ancestor. Whether or not Ashton really believes the story of Malise Ravenswood's revenge is beside the point. The point is that Ashton associates the relatively weak antagonist of the present with the deadly enemy of a past which is, at least partly, fictive, with an enemy who survives only in local tradition.

Ashton's relationship with the son of his old adversary reproduces in small a key pattern in Scott's exploitation of the Gothic. From Ashton's perspective, the penniless and dispossessed heir of a dying aristocratic family, a figure existing on the margins of the novel's social world, takes on a disruptive force which is embellished by a filial connection with an aristocrat of ancient legend. Ashton's scheme for a reconciliation with Ravenswood is a means of controlling the threat posed by Ravenswood's combination of pedigree, aristocratic temper, and connections and of using his enemy's strength to his own advantage. Scott's early presentation of Ravenswood invests the figure with a certain disruptive force. But with its repeated and consistent gestures of domestication, its transformation of the Gothic hero/villain into a figure of moderation, its translation of supernatural elements into the reassuring language of psychological analysis, the novel deprives its feudal aristocrat, and the barbaric past which the figure evokes, of the very power it has granted.

We might say simply that *The Bride* evokes in its aristocratic hero a figure of demonic force in order to purge that force from its world.[26] But the effects of the novel, like its fictional modes, are strangely mixed, and cannot be so easily sorted out. With its weird amalgam of genres, *The Bride* is shaped by contradictory political motives: a wish for the restoration of the old landed establishment, and the imperative of ratifying the very property relations which prevent the fulfillment of that wish. The novel's allegiances are deeply divided between the necessity of assimilating and containing the disruptive force embodied in its feudal figures, and a desire, at once subversive and reactionary, for the revitalization of the feudal social order.

Scott's appropriation of the emotionally potent mythologies of Gothic romance serves two distinct ideological ends. Scott describes a consciousness for his feudal characters which is ideological in the narrow sense, that is, a false consciousness which is subject to demystification by the novel's narrating voice. At the same time, his strategies confer an effect of supernatural fatality on the novel's realistic elements which confirms the necessity of the feudal aristocracy's demise. Scott deploys the Gothic in order to expose it as the irrational and therefore false consciousness of a moribund feudal order, as he places the myth of supernatural necessity in the service of his realism. These strategies reinforce the simple historical lesson which we find repeatedly in the Waverley novels, that the demise of the traditional aristocratic order is an unfortunate, but necessary, concomitant of progress. But this is only one side of the story. Closely linked with the novel's realistic social and psychological analysis is a fantasy of landed establishment. Against the powerful imperative of historical progress, the novel registers a nostalgia for the presumably happier arrangements of a feudal Scotland, a Scotland dominated by the powerful and warlike barons who held the Ravenswood estate in centuries past. Edgar Ravenswood is the most prominent instance of the dualism which pervades the novel. Ravenswood's consciousness shifts back and forth between two registers, between a vision of history as a powerful and destructive fatality, and as an opportunity, difficult and dangerous, to gain a place within the new social order. Beginning like a romance hero, in a state of innocence and ignorance, Ravenswood is confronted with a series of physical and moral ordeals which he must survive in order to attain a niche in the class which has displaced his once dominant ancestors. The paradox of Ravenswood's position in the novel is that he must use the opportunity which history presents to him in order to escape the fatality with which history threatens him. His greatest ordeal as hero of Scott's historical romance is to survive the vicissitudes of history and somehow achieve a position of transcendence which places him outside of history. He must accept the conditions which history has forced upon him in order to escape the destruction which history has visited upon his ancestors.

After a long dialogue with Ashton at Wolf's Crag, Ravenswood considers the possibility of a reconciliation with his father's enemy:

... if he is willing to adjust even his acknowledged rights upon an equitable footing, what could be my father's cause of complaint? – what is mine? – Those from whom we won our ancient possessions fell under the sword of my ancestors, and left lands and living to the conquerors; we sink under the force of the law, now too powerful for the Scottish chivalry. Let us parley with the victors of the day, as if we had been besieged in our fortress, and without hope of relief. This man may have been other than I thought him; and his daughter ...   (ch. 14; 221–22)

These are the "calmer thoughts," the deliberations that follow the "tempest of passion" in a shift between the irrational and the rational which is the typical pattern of Ravenswood's perceptions. Ravenswood has heard Ashton's persuasive entreaties for a reconciliation, and finds himself caught in a bind:

His mortal foe was under his roof, yet his sentiments towards him were neither those of a feudal enemy nor of a true Christian. He felt as if he could neither forgive him in the one character, nor follow forth his vengeance in the other, but that he was making a base and dishonourable composition betwixt his resentment against the father and his affection for his daughter.

(ch. 14; 221)

In this instant of passion immediately following the colloquy with Ashton, the terms of the dilemma become clear. Ravenswood's allegiance to the feudal past requires vengeance against his father's enemy. Yet there is a contrary pull, the palliative force of his incipient affection for the enemy's daughter. The ambivalence registered here is resolved, for a brief moment, in the "calmer thoughts" which come after. When the moment of passion has passed, Ravenswood reconsiders the events which have led to his family's decline. Recognizing that his own family's ascendance was achieved through violence, he views the fall of the Ravenswoods within the larger perspective of Scottish history. What he arrives at in his "place of repose" is a condition of balance and moderation, a disposition toward past and present in which reconciliation with the man who had been his father's "mortal foe" (ch. 14; 221) becomes an acceptable course of action.

But the equilibrium established here proves fragile, while the ambivalence persists practically from the beginning to the novel's end. At the opening of the novel, Ravenswood is a Gothic hero, attired in the requisite black, declaring his intention to confront the usurper in appropriately archaic language. In the impassioned speech which he makes after his father's funeral, Ravenswood represents himself as the last and seemingly doomed member of an ancient feudal house. Yet when his arch-enemy is threatened by one of the wild bulls remaining on the estate from the heyday of the Ravenswoods, he intervenes as a protector (ch. 5; 65–70). The scene in which Ravenswood kills the bull acquires an allegorical, as well as a supernatural, dimension in the light of the ancient legend of Malise Ravenswood's revenge. Scott's insistent allegorizing forces us to interpret the bull's attack as an expression of the hostility of the feudal estate, of which Ravenswood is the sole surviving representative, towards the interloper, a hostility which is then suppressed by the central feudal figure. By shooting the bull, Ravenswood subdues, for an instant, the threat of the past, and rescues his enemy from danger.

But there is more to the scene than political allegory. Ravenswood's failure to perform his sworn vow of revenge results from his sudden attraction to Lucy, an attraction which will eventually bring him back to the house of his feudal ancestors as a suitor of his enemy's daughter.

Ravenswood's affection for Lucy will soon become a crucial force in shaping his thoughts and actions. With this shift, the subversive energy of Ravenswood, originally directed at his family's bourgeois antagonist, is momentarily subdued within the form of a courtship.

At work here is the process of domestication which began in the opening scene. To the psychologizing pattern established there, the novel joins an ethical discourse in which Ravenswood will appear as both subject and object, as a figure who chooses his own course of action and whose choices are, in turn, judged from an "objective" vantage point outside of the action. As he approaches Lucy Ashton at the Mermaiden's Well, Ravenswood considers the conflict in which his relationship with his enemy's daughter has placed him:

> The pleasure he felt in Lucy's company had indeed approached to fascination, yet it had never altogether surmounted his internal reluctance to wed with the daughter of his father's foe ... Still, he felt that Alice spoke the truth, and that his honour required that he should take an instant leave of Ravenswood Castle, or become a suitor of Lucy Ashton.   (ch. 20; 288)

Old Alice's dire prognostications about the consequences of his attachment to Lucy play an important part in shaping the movement of Ravenswood's thoughts. But at this moment Alice's message is not the determining force in his decision, but merely one element of a dilemma defined through Ravenswood's consciousness.

In the earlier scene at Wolf's Crag, the novel had shown a figure with a complicated interior life, a passional life divorced from the concrete realities of its social and historical situation. By the time Ravenswood approaches the Mermaiden's Well, he has been granted a self-reflexive faculty which enables him to exercise control over his conflicting passions. While he is conscious of his fascination with Lucy, he still harbors an aversion to a union with the family of his father's *arriviste* enemy and allows a certain element of veracity to Alice's prophecies. With Alice's warning of doom still fresh in his mind, Ravenswood hesitates for a moment at the place "where two paths parted" (ch. 20; 288). If he takes the path towards the Well, he risks a potentially fatal entanglement with the Ashton family; if he takes the other, he may survive. Scott's symbolism here is transparent and clumsy. But the point is that Ravenswood is drawn as an ordinary human, facing a moral dilemma and weighing his choices.

The legend attached to the fountain impinges on Ravenswood's consciousness during his conversation with Lucy: "It has been thought ... a fatal spot to my family" (ch. 20; 290). But the editorial tone of the novel's narrating voice militates against a supernatural reading of the incident:

To a superstitious eye, Lucy Ashton, folded in her plaided mantle, with her long hair, escaping partly from the snood and falling upon her silver neck, might have suggested the murdered Nymph of the Fountain. But Ravenswood saw only a female exquisitely beautiful, and rendered yet more so in his eyes – how could it be otherwise? – by the consciousness that she had placed her affections on him.   (ch. 20; 289)

The passage places beside one another two ways of seeing, the supernatural and the rational, and quietly, but firmly, ratifies the latter. As George Levine has pointed out, "The 'superstitious eye' might have been valuable here, but the rhetoric does not endorse superstition."[27] Ravenswood's gestures in this scene are to be regarded as the result of his own choice, rather than of the pattern of fatality embodied in the family legend.

To the "superstitious eye," the scene at the Well would appear a repetition of an old pattern of love and murder from which the Ravenswoods have suffered since ancient times. Accordingly, Ravenswood and his lover would merely be passive vehicles in a cyclical pattern of family history shaped by a supernatural fatality, modern versions of the original nymph and her murderous lover. But the disparity between the nymph of legend and the daughter of the Lord Keeper is registered in Lucy's literary effusions over the place of their meeting: "I like this spot ... the bubbling murmur of the clear fountain, the waving of trees, the profusion of grass and wild-flowers, that rise among the ruins." Viewed by a mind nourished on tales of chivalry, the meeting at the Well appears "like a scene in romance" (ch. 20; 290).

Scott emphasizes Lucy's literary predilections, and shapes her reading of events accordingly. Susceptible to feelings of a "romantic cast," Lucy takes "secret delight" in "legendary tales of ardent devotion and unalterable affection." Scott clearly wants the reader to regard Lucy's perception of things as unrealistic, a matter of fancy and delusion. Her vision of Edgar Ravenswood is a product of imaginative activity, of an art which can only be practiced in the privacy of her "retired chamber" or the "woodland bower she had chosen for her own and called after her name ..." (ch. 3; 45). Lucy's romancing is an essentially subjective activity, the solitary exercise of an imagination that creates a world after its own image.

In one significant respect, Lucy's vision coincides with the feudal consciousness embodied in the Ravenswood legends. Those "old legendary tales" in which Lucy takes delight are "chequered ... with strange adventures and supernatural horrors" (ch. 3; 45), a generic description which neatly fits the stories of the Mermaiden's Well and Malise Ravenswood's revenge, along with the peasant's account of events given in the opening scene. But the figure of Lucy is a curious hybrid, another instance of the novel's ambivalent vision. As a daydreamer who entertains herself with supernatural tales and romances of chivalry, she is aligned with the irrational and deluded consciousness which informs that literature. In Lucy's pleas to Ravenswood that he delay revealing their betrothal to her father, however, the other side comes into play.

Lucy's affair with Ravenswood has both a private and a social dimension. The strength of her emotion has its source in the private dimension, the life of imagination which is lived in the secrecy of bedroom and bower. But her passion for "old legendary tales" and her affection for Ravenswood are proscribed by a reality principle which is vague in shape, but very powerful. In her private life, Lucy engages in all manner of sentimental excess, doing whatever she wishes. But in "her exterior relations to things of this world, Lucy willingly received the ruling impulse from those around her." While Ravenswood is a source of secret delight, in the social world of "exterior relations," he is not much of a prize. Outside of Lucy's "fairy realm" (ch. 3; 45), Ravenswood is an indigent and propertyless aristocrat, a feudal lord without land or vassals, the holder of a mere courtesy title. Lacking the financial and property qualifications for marriage into a wealthy family ambitious to improve its social and political position, Ravenswood can only be a successful suitor in the literary realm of romance.

Scott's handling of the betrothal is intended to show that the reconciliation of new money with old landed blood is a historical impossibility, a mere daydream with no more force in reality than Lucy Ashton's romancing. Yet in his description of Lucy and Edgar's love, Scott indulges in the kind of imaginative activity which he appears to reject. The lovers' feelings for one another seem to have

little to do with the difficult issues of class relations. Their love is
described as if it occurred mainly in a realm of emotional and physical
attraction, a world of sentiment superior to social and political
realities. Yet this realm is also clearly literary, the artificial world of
romance. Even as Scott establishes the possibility of a happy union,
he suggests that the relationship of Edgar and Lucy is founded on
delusion; he projects a resolution to the social and political conflicts
which he has described, and then proves that this resolution cannot
succeed. The union of the old order with the new must fail, based
as it is on imaginative constructions divorced from external reality,
from the determining world of social and historical relations.

One would like to say that at this point Scott is being relentlessly
realistic in showing the necessary failure of a reconciliation between
the declining feudal aristocracy and the rising bourgeoisie. Setting
aside the issue of theoretical naiveté, a reading of the novel premised
on its historical veracity fails even on its own criteria. To speak of
a pure form of feudal aristocracy existing in residual form somewhere
on the southeastern coast of Scotland, or, for that matter, anywhere
else in the Kingdom near the beginning of the eighteenth century, is
to ignore historical realities which Scott himself tacitly acknowledges.[28] The decline of the feudal aristocracy in Scotland and
England had begun long before the exile of James II and was well
advanced by the time of the Union. By the Lukácsian standard of
typicality, the grasping and willful Lady Ashton, scion of a younger
branch of the Douglas family, would be a far more representative
figure of the Scottish nobility than Edgar Ravenswood. If *The Bride*
was written as a lament for the feudal order of ancient Scotland, it
was rather belated.

The most fascinating feature of the novel is not its historical
content, but its mingling of a historical narrative about the relations
between classes with a complex love story, its intertwining of political
allegory with sexual fantasy. Scott's ambivalence in *The Bride* is at
once political and sexual. We have isolated one of the novel's wish-
fulfilling registers in the vision of a restored landed aristocracy, a wish
held out and then thwarted in the figure of Ravenswood. Extending
and modifying Shaw's biographical reading,[29] we can see in the
novel's sexual subplot a sado-masochistic impulse. Ravenswood's
relationship with Lucy Ashton expresses a desire for upward mobility,
a wish which is blocked in the novel. At the same time, the dream of

landed establishment, that fantasy narrative in which the hero and heroine inherit great tracts of property and live happily ever after, is enacted and defeated. Linked with the novel's political register is the sexual narrative of a rejected lover's fantasy of revenge.

These patterns repeat the Belsches episode (see p. 10 above), but with important strategic variations, the most significant of which is an alteration in the class affiliations of the suitor and the woman whose hand he seeks. At the age of twenty-four, Scott was Williamina Belsches's social inferior, the son of a Scottish lawyer with limited connections. In *The Bride*, written almost twenty-five years later, Ravenswood is the dispossessed heir of a noble estate. The primary enemy of his suit is the wife of a conniving Whig lawyer, a parvenu who tries to use her distant connections with the Douglas family as an instrument of advancement.

Ravenswood's return at the very moment in which Lucy is to sign the marriage contract with Bucklaw is a double-edged act of vengeance. In drawing his weapons and threatening violence against the gathering, Ravenswood is punishing the family which has usurped his lordly prerogatives and debased his reputation by spurning his proposal of marriage. But the ambivalence registered in the betrothal scene at the Mermaiden's Well persists here. Ravenswood returns to his ancestral home not to reenact the bloodbath of Malise Ravenswood's revenge, but, by his own declaration, to determine his fiancée's real disposition. His threats of violence remain threats. Edgar's version of Malise's revenge involves at once an assault on the bourgeois enemy who has stolen his lands and rejected his offer of alliance, and on the unregenerate aristocrat who, at his father's funeral, had pronounced a deadly curse against the usurper of his patrimonial rights. Trapped in duality, Ravenswood becomes, in the very gesture of attacking Lady Ashton, party to her torture of Lucy. His operatic entry into the hall and his demand that he will hear Lucy's "determination from her own mouth" (ch. 33; 462) augment Lady Ashton's torment of her daughter, contributing to the triumph she had sought over Ravenswood and the revenge which the aristocrat in Ravenswood so passionately desired.

Notably absent from these final chapters of the novel is a social symbol which would resolve the antinomies of class and temperament brought to focus in the scene of Ravenswood's return. The felicitous union implied in the betrothal of Edgar Ravenswood and Lucy Ashton is thwarted by the machinations of Lady Ashton. In the gory wedding-night scene which follows the forced match of Lucy and Bucklaw, Ravenswood's betrothed is reduced to a gibbering madwoman, an "exulting demoniac" dabbled with the blood of her own groom (ch. 34; 483). Scott's deviation from a common convention of his own work thus eliminates an essential unifying symbol. The closing chapters of *Waverley* describe, in contrast, the bestowal of prosperity upon husband and wife and their elevation to a position of stability on a restored feudal estate. By marrying his errant hero to the daughter of a Scottish aristocrat and elevating the couple into prosperity, Scott fixes at once Waverley's position within the social structure of the novel and his relation to the feudal order of the past and the dominant order of the present. The union of estates and nations projected at the close of *Waverley* implies that the turbulent movements of history can be controlled, that its conflicts can be resolved through a common social gesture. The marriage of Edward Waverley and Rose Bradwardine guarantees at least some limited accommodation for the old order within the new. Baron Bradwardine will presumably pass his final years on a Tully-Veolan estate restored through the munificence of his son-in-law.

Waverley represents an effort to strike a balance between the rise of the new order and the decline of the old, to find virtue on both sides of the struggle. But in place of a happy compromise between past and present, *The Bride* conveys a dark vision of historical change, enacting the betrayal and destruction of its lovers and sounding a powerful lament for the passing of traditional ways. Edward Waverley's purchase of Tully-Veolan and his marriage to the scion of a noble Scottish family represent precisely what is never accomplished in *The Bride*, the assimilation and preservation of the disenfranchised aristocracy. The novel ends without achieving historical balance. The decline of the traditional order, validated in *Waverley* by the emergence of a new and benevolent order, becomes an occasion for profound regret. Only the vicious and implacable Lady Ashton survives at the end, living on to "the verge of extreme old age" (ch. 30; 408).

Yet the scenes of social life at Wolf's Hope stand as an answer to the mood of pessimism which dominates Scott's presentation of the Ravenswoods' decline. Once a part of the Ravenswoods' demesne, Wolf's Hope is an image of the new Scotland in microcosm, of the society which has emerged from and now superseded the feudal order represented in the ruined castle at Wolf's Crag. Describing the villagers' experience of their new condition, Scott observes that

They resembled a prisoner that has been long fettered, who even at liberty, feels in imagination the grasp of the handcuffs still binding his wrist. But the exercise of freedom is quickly followed with the natural consciousness of its immunities, as the enlarged prisoner, by the free use of his limbs, soon dispels the cramped feeling they had acquired when bound. (ch. 12; 186)

What appeals to the villagers, to the self-employed fishermen and tradesmen of Wolf's Hope, is a bourgeois ideology of proprietorship. Caleb Balderstone's conception of the ties binding Wolf's Hope to Wolf's Crag is sadly out of accord with the villagers' changed sense of their relationship to the Ravenswoods. When Caleb requisitions butter and eggs for Wolf's Crag, invoking the ancient rights of his master, the villagers organize themselves to resist the exaction. Their claim of emancipation is made succinctly by one of the "Conscript Fathers of the village": "Their hens had caickled mony a day for the Lords of Ravenswood, and it was time they suld caickle for those that gave them roosts and barley" (ch. 12; 187). The head of the insurrection is Gibbie Girder, the prosperous cooper from whose hearth Caleb pilfers a dinner on the night of the Ashtons' visit to Wolf's Crag. Whatever satirical element may be present in Scott's treatment of the cooper, the scene which Caleb discovers on his foray into the village is the "Reverse of the sad menage at the Castle of Wolf's Crag" (ch. 12; 193). The cooper's apartment is large and comfortable, and its proprietor enjoys a mastery there of which the henpecked Lord Keeper is deprived, for "he was not of that class of lords and masters whose wives are viceroys over them" (ch. 12; 203). In contrast to the dark solitude of Wolf's Crag, the cooper's house is a place where a large and active family gathers for substantial meals, where babies are christened, and a jovial young housewife presides over the hearth. This is the closest the novel will approach to a positive representation of social life and, as such, is an argument against the gloomy vision conveyed in the novel's description of Ravenswood's career.

Scott's critique of the new order is countered not only by his depiction of the cooper's family, but by his satirizing of aristocratic values, a satire focused on the figure of Caleb Balderstone. Compelled by the need to preserve appearances in the face of the family's decline,

Caleb resorts to a series of transparent subterfuges. To give his master an alibi for failing to provide his distinguished guests with an appropriate meal, Caleb wrecks the kitchen at Wolf's Crag and claims that the damage was done by a bolt of lightning. To disguise the embarrassing condition of Ravenswood's pantry, he steals a goose from the prosperous cooper of Wolf's Hope. And to drive away any other visitors who might see Wolf's Crag in its real state of degeneracy, he sets fire to the straw in the courtyard.

The figure of Caleb could be explained simply as a comic personification of the virtues and absurdities of the old order. But Caleb's gestures are too comical, too absurd to serve mainly as a way of establishing critical balance. Caleb's drive to keep up appearances lifts the figure out of the novel's realistic account of the Ravenswoods' decline into the generic realm of comic caricature. The figure of Caleb must be seen not only as a piece of satire, but as an evasive response to the novel's historical action, a means of diverting the reader's attention from the depressing spectacle of Ravenswood's poverty. Like a Caleb conscious of his own effects, Scott uses comical tricks to help keep up appearances, to distract the reader from the social conditions which he has himself soberly recorded. In the scene depicting the Ashtons' visit to Wolf's Crag, what could have been merely a degrading exhibition of Ravenswood's indigence becomes an occasion for both humiliation and laughter, with Scott prescribing his readers' responses through the mixed reactions of his characters (ch. 11; 173–78).

Rather than try to resolve the conflicting interpretative possibilities of *The Bride* into a unitary progressive or reactionary reading, we must regard the novel's formal disjunctions as signs of a deeper motivating force. The meaning of the novel is not merely a set of propositions about history, but a process of transformation. The novel signifies by reworking unsavory or threatening fantasies into intellectual, social, and moral themes – hence the presentation of social life at Wolf's Hope, with its nascent individualism and economic prosperity against the poverty and decay of Wolf's Crag, the crumbling haven of the feudal order, and the double-edged satire of bourgeois and aristocratic values. Hence also the novel's reiterated arguments against the feudal way of understanding: its assertion of the primacy of rational consciousness over superstition and of determinate material causes over supernatural forces; its crude empiricist epistemology, in which a rational subject perceives and registers an objective world which works according to laws of cause and effect. In its demystification of the supernatural, its rejections of romance and its exploitation of romance forms, its comparisons of traditional and modern social orders, the novel presents to its reader a legible text, relatively unified and coherent. This legible text is the text as ideology, serving to conceal the contradictions registered in the fantasy narrative enfolded within it. By its presentation of such thematic problems as the troubled relationship of past and present, the necessary yet regrettable decline of feudal virtues, the inadequacy of romance as a way of perceiving reality, the novel disguises the political fantasies which it simultaneously enacts.[30]

4

REDGAUNTLET: THE HISTORICAL ROMANCE AS METAFICTION

Some five years after writing his nightmare vision of historical change in *The Bride*, Scott returns in *Redgauntlet* to the problems of representation he had first touched on in *Waverley*, and which he had made the dominant issue of *Old Mortality*. Here again, the immediate subject of the novel is an unsuccessful rebellion. But *Redgauntlet* is about a rebellion that never occurred. By eliding the historical referent he had supplied in the earlier novels, Scott shifts the emphasis of his writing, to a greater degree than ever, towards the processes of making historical narrative. He makes the fact of the novel's fictionality its defining feature, not simply underscoring his own contrivances, but using his "romantic history," as his young lawyer Alan Fairford would have it, of the Redgauntlet family as the pretext for an elaborate study of his own methods as historian and romancer.

The amiable and detached commentary on his own fictions we find in *Waverley*, the demystifying thrusts and playful self-parodies of *Old Mortality*, are incorporated in *Redgauntlet* into Scott's deceptively casual remarks on the power and limitations of his fictions as instruments for grasping the movements of history. In *Waverley*, Scott's reflections on his procedures of depicting the past are contained within the narrative itself, stated directly in brief discursive passages and implicitly in Scott's handling of various representational devices – pictures, letters, gazette reports. History is defined as the effect available to the reader through a series of distances, accessible only at a multiple remove, through the mediating forms of legends, romances, family histories. *Old Mortality* reflects Scott's preoccupation with the role of historically determined languages on human actions, the force of the symbols generated in historical struggle, of class-bound languages, in shaping the course of history. Scott presents a layering of editors whose statements the reader must sift through and weigh against one another in the process of making his own interpretation of the narrative. The reader's access to the past is always mediated by one of Scott's editor-figures, first the author, then Jedidiah Cleisbotham, then Peter Pattieson.[1] Rather than distancing his reader from the past through layers of memory, Scott works as he does in *Waverley*, by placing distancing devices within the narrative itself. Instead of Cleisbotham's bombast and Pattieson's qualifications of his modest project, Scott uses the strategies of epistolary correspondence, third-person narration, and the personal journal. The letters that take up most of the first third of the novel present two narrators – setting aside for the moment Blind Willie Ste'enson – each interpreting the materials drawn from the other's letters, from local lore, and from second-hand accounts of events. Cleisbotham and Pattieson are thus supplanted by Darsie and Alan, whose letters are collected by Dr. Dryasdust and then passed on to the "Author of Waverley." In a gesture apparently designed to help the reader comprehend the larger view of things, Scott inserts a third figure, a proper third-person narrator, who, if we are to judge from Scott's claims, is to be regarded as impartial. But the subjective nature of the epistolary method reduces the credibility of the third-person narration. We apprehend the events of the novel through the changing vision of the two friends alternately; and it is only after their perceptions have led them, and us, to a secluded corner of Dumfriesshire that we receive the benefit of the narrator's fuller understanding. Introduced in the middle of the story as a kind of annotation of the letters, the account of Scott's third-person narrator underscores the essential subjectivity of the novel's content thus far. The reader seeking the facts about Darsie's experiences at Solway can only read his own version of events into the dialogue between Darsie and Alan. Until Scott inserts his narrator to sort the matter out, the reader must work after the fashion of Pattieson in *Old Mortality*, attempting to correct the biassed account of the one with counter-assertions and scraps of information drawn from the other.[2]

The problem of sorting out fact from fiction seems simple enough at the beginning of the novel, when Darsie has just departed from the safe confines of the Fairfords' home in Edinburgh to seek adventure on the road. Darsie appears at this moment as the personification of fancy as compared to Alan's fact, imagination to reason, romance to novel.[3] Their letters are moments in the generic dialogue that animates Scott's fiction from the earliest work. That Scott continued to write this conversation, even later in his career, suggests the power of romance as a shaping force in his conception of historical fiction. Scott imagined the writing of historical fiction as a mixture of these two apparently conflicting genres, as the product of an ongoing argument between two ways of seeing, which could be resolved only by the victory of one over the other, or by a third term Scott never clearly defined, and that perhaps was never fully conceived.

The extended pieces of historical reportage which appear throughout the Waverley novels place Scott in the company of Defoe. But Scott's self-conscious playing with the procedures of historical representation anticipate a more modern preoccupation with the power and limits of the imagination as an instrument for writing history and with the problematic relationship between language and reality. Scott is at his most modern in *Redgauntlet*, where the accurate observation of historical conditions is deemphasized in favor of metafictional reflection. The epistolary technique used in the first part of the novel would seem to reflect Scott's indebtedness to his eighteenth-century predecessors. But the sequence of letters is broken off abruptly with a brief discourse on the relative merits of third-person narration and "epistolary correspondence." Scott not only announces the shift in technique to the reader, thus calling attention to the novel's design, but offers a rationale for the change:

The advantage of laying before the reader, in the words of the actors themselves, the adventures which we must otherwise have narrated in our own, has given great popularity to the publication of epistolary correspondence, as practiced by various great authors, and by ourselves in the preceding chapters. Nevertheless, a genuine correspondence of this kind (and Heaven forbid it should be in any respect sophisticated by interpolations of our own!) can seldom be found to contain all in which it is necessary to instruct the reader for his full comprehension of the story. Also it must happen that various prolixities and redundancies occur in an interchange of letters, which must hang as a dead weight on the progress of the narrative ... the course of storytelling which we have for the present adopted, resembles the original discipline of the dragoons, who were trained to serve either on foot or horseback, as emergencies of the service required. With this explanation, we shall proceed to narrate some circumstances which Alan Fairford did not, and could not, write to his correspondent.   (ch. 1; 235–36)

Scott's interpolation suggests, somewhat disingenuously, that his reason for using the epistolary form was its popular appeal. Ever mindful of public tastes, Scott no doubt considered the value of pleasing his audience in designing the correspondence of Darsie and Alan. But more importantly, he points here to a significant deficiency of the personal letter as a method of storytelling. The "genuine correspondence" which he has just exhibited to the reader does not, and cannot, encompass all of the information which the reader will require for "full comprehension" of the story. Even in the context of Scott's bluff and easygoing discussion of his method, "full comprehension" carries considerable weight. Scott shifts from the personal letter to third-person narration because he needs to convey to his reader "particulars" concerning the principal characters of the story which might otherwise remain beyond the reader's grasp. Scott's narrator will provide a comprehensive account of characters and events against the subjective perceptions registered in the letters of Darsie and Alan. In taking a step to advance the progress of the story, Scott allows his reader to catch up with the movement of events, but also to evaluate the perceptions expressed in the letters from a vantage point outside of the dialogue, making the reader, at least for the moment, the epistemological equal of the narrator.

Scott's shift in technique allows the reader to share in the narrator's perspective. His announcement of that shift is a statement to the reader of the author's power to alter the form of presentation as he will, to change his method according to the demands of the story which he has conceived. In the process of storytelling, Scott not only gives the reader a fuller comprehension of things, but creates another version of events. The author's intervention at this moment is a way of unifying the disparate perspectives elaborated in the fictive correspondence of Darsie and Alan. The voice of the third-person narrator is the synthesizing voice of the fabulist, of the mythmaker whose vision raises the novel above the level of subjective speculation. Yet the third-person perspective is also just another way of seeing things, "direct narrative" as opposed to "epistolary correspondence." It is a device of storytelling, a trick from the romancer's bag, more convenient under the circumstances than the epistolary technique. The narrator's view provides not an objective version of things as they were, but rather a comprehensive story about what has happened and why things happened the way they did, against which the subjective views of Darsie and Alan can be measured. The "romantic history" composed by Darsie in his search for his paternal origins is another such hypothesis. In his first letter, Alan reminds Darsie of the latter's propensity for concocting improbable narratives and placing himself at the center:

But what dost thou look to? The chance that the mystery, as you call it, which at present overclouds your birth and connexions, will clear up into something inexpressibly and inconceivably brilliant; and this without any effort of your own, but purely by the good-will of Fortune. I know the pride and the naughtiness of thy heart and sincerely do I wish that thou hadst more beatings to thank me for than those which thou dost acknowledge so gratefully. Then had I thumped these Quixotical expectations out of thee, and thou hadst not, as now, conceived thyself to be the hero of some romantic history, and converted in thy vain imagination honest Griffiths, citizen and broker, who never bestows more than the needful upon his quarterly epistles, into some wise Alexander or sage Alquife, the mystical and magical protector of thy peerless destiny.   (Letter 2; 25–26)

Writing as if he were a self-conscious verson of Sancho Panza, thumping out the Quixotical tendencies and thumping in the facts, Alan warns his friend to avoid the delusions of self-made fictions, providing a small reminder of reality in his corrective description of Griffiths. The passage establishes a central pattern in the dialogue between Alan and Darsie. Alan is the voice of things as they are, inveighing against the romantic imagination, exhorting his friend to keep his fancy under control. He is an eminently practical young man, trying to keep his friend's feet on the ground. In the generic terms established by Scott in his "Essay on Romance" (1824), Alan is at this moment the voice of the novel, endorsing the "ordinary train of events" against the fanciful productions of romance.[4]

In its early passages, *Redgauntlet* looks very much like *Waverley*, with Darsie standing in for Edward Waverley as the hero of romantic imagination, seemingly another prime candidate for the pattern of delusion and disenchantment established in the earlier novel. What Scott has attempted in the first part of *Redgauntlet* is to recast the familiar material of *Waverley* in epistolary form, with the aim of extending and complicating his reflections on the relationship between historical fiction and history. In *Waverley*, romance and history appear as opposed tendencies in the consciousness of a single character, with romance predominant in the opening chapters. Scott's rewriting of the *Waverley* material in 1824 involves the division of these guiding tendencies into the voices of two separate characters, engaged in an amiable and yet serious argument over what precisely is the truth of the events before them. His purpose is to place the issue of presentation which he had thematized overtly in his first novel at the center of *Redgauntlet*. He accomplishes this by squaring off the two dominant genres of his writing in a cleverly composed verbal contest, a sparring match which has no clear victor.

Darsie's description of his adventure on the Solway sands resembles Waverley's transformation of the Scottish landscape on his approach to Tully-Veolan. Preparing the prosaic mind of his friend for the reception of his story, Darsie renders the setting sun as "a warrior prepared for defence," showing his "ruddy front ... over a huge battlemented and turreted wall of crimson and black clouds, which appeared like an immense Gothic fortress, into which the lord of day was descending" (Letter 4; 40). Mounted behind his rescuer, Darsie will find in the shadow of the horse and rider a reminder of the "Magician Atlantes on his hippogriff, with a knight trussed up behind him, in the manner Ariosto has depicted that matter" (Letter 4; 47). In these moments of imaginative excess, Darsie's language sounds like the gushing of a pretentious adolescent, and the reader is ready to plead along with Alan, "View things as they are, and not as they may be magnified through thy teeming fancy" (Letter 2; 27).

But Darsie's letter is only a single, relatively brief moment in the correspondence, representing one position in the extended dialogue between him and Alan. Darsie renders his rescuer in the manner of Ariosto. Yet he then describes the cottage of his host in the shorthand of the "philosophical" historian which Scott had used in the scene of Edward Waverley's entry into Tully-Veolan village:

There was something about all that I saw which seemed to intimate, that I was rather in the abode of a decayed gentleman, who clung to a few of the forms and observances of a former rank, than in that of a common peasant, raised above his fellows by comparative opulence.　　　　(Letter 4; 52)

Following these observations on the social status and economic condition of his host, Darsie gives a detailed description of the cottage's interior, including the arrangement of pewter and earthenware and the quality of the furnishings. Despite his proclivities to fancy, Darsie is astute enough to notice in the events of the day a "mysterious incongruity" and to detect in the abode of a "fisher" tell-tale signs of an uncharacteristic affluence. But along with Darsie's close attention to seemingly "trivial and ordinary circumstances" (Letter 4; 53) is his propensity for placing the objects of his reflections within the schema of a grand story of heroic action. Describing the manner and dress of his host, Darsie writes:

His shirt was without ruffles, and tied at the collar with a black ribband, which showed his strong and muscular neck rising from it, like that of an ancient Hercules ... I could not help running mentally over the ancient heroes, to whom I might assimilate the noble form and countenance before me. He was too young, and evinced too little resignation to his fate, to resemble Belisarius. Coriolanus standing by the hearth of Tullus Aufidius came nearer the mark; yet the gloomy and haughty look of the stranger had, perhaps, still more of Marius seated among the ruins of Carthage.   (Letter 4; 54)

Darsie's "imaginations," ill-founded though they are at this instant, receive some limited encouragement from Alan's letter. Fairford opens with a piece of deft mockery: "Wert thou to plant the bean in the nursery tale, thou wouldst make out, soon as it had begun to germinate, that the castle of the giant was about to elevate its battlements on the top of it" (Letter 5; 65). Darsie's letter is thus consigned to the world of the "nursery tale." But Alan's own letter will become a rich source of material for Darsie's imagination and a stimulus to the curiosity of the reader. Alan closes the letter with a warning against "castle-building" on the basis of the information he has given:

Adieu! and although I have given thee a subject for waking dreams, beware of building a castle too heavy for the foundation; which, in the present instance, is barely the word "Latimer" occurring in a conversation betwixt a gentleman of Dumfriesshire and a W.S. of Edinburgh. *Coetera prorsus ignoro.*   (Letter 5; 78)

Alan knows very well that his information is bound to pique his friend's curiosity. This recognition places him and, by implication, the reader, in a role closer to Darsie's than his first letter would suggest. Darsie's rendering of his experience at Solway was subjected to the skeptical interpretation of his friend. But now, the practical and hardheaded young advocate assumes, for the moment, the opposite part in the dialogue. Now Darsie, along with the reader, must sort out the mysterious circumstances of Mr. Herries's visit to

Edinburgh. The dropping of the name "Latimer" by Saunders Fairford, wadded about by Alan's warnings against "building a hundred castles in the air," creates an enigma, a puzzle which acquires greater portent with Alan's dismissals of its significance.

Alan chides Darsie for his account of the rescue, mocking what he conceives to be the pure products of fancy: "Didst ever see what artists call a Claude Lorraine glass, which spreads its own particular hue over the whole landscape which you see through it? Thou beholdest ordinary events through just such a medium." His response to Darsie's story is a jocular admonition against "making histories out of nothing" (Letter 5; 65), against spreading the "particular hue" of imagination over a very ordinary train of events. But in his effort to describe Mr. Herries, Alan himself begins to paint a picture of his subject:

> If I had thy power of imagination and description, Darsie, I could make out a fine, dark, mysterious, Rembrandt-looking portrait of this same stranger, which should be as far superior to thy fisherman as a shirt of chain-mail is to a herring-net.   (Letter 5; 74–75)

Alan insists that the "stranger" who came to consult with his father is not to be identified with Darsie's "fisherman." In suggesting what a portrait of the man might look like, he creates a pictorial enigma, and at the same time, mocks his own creation. We have seen Darsie puzzle over the social status of his rescuer, and then, drawing on his stock of heroic myths and legends, attempt to explain the man's mysterious features, with comical results. Now Alan introduces in his letter a strange gentleman who goes by the name of Herries, but provides only a few vague clues as to the stranger's purpose in visiting Mr. Fairford.

Scott is hinting here at the approaching convergence of the two worlds which he has established thus far in the correspondence. Alan lives in the "real" world of upper-middle-class Edinburgh society, where "you cannot mistake the character of those you converse with, or suffer your fancy to exaggerate their qualities ... without exposing yourself not only to ridicule, but to great and serious inconveniences" (Letter 2; 28). Alan's language implies that it is possible and even necessary to assess a character at a determinate value. In Darsie's vision, a fisherman is transformed into a Hercules or a Coriolanus. But Alan's assessment of Mr. Herries will prove to be simply one limited perspective on a figure of seemingly Protean powers. If Darsie's rescuer is no Hercules, neither is he merely a pretentious old crank of Jacobitical tendencies. Even in Alan's professedly realistic vision, Herries remains something of a mystery, and becomes an object of speculation.

Scott's attitude toward the romantic imagination is implied in Darsie's use of a legal metaphor to describe his relationship with Alan. Darsie's first letter is taken up largely with recollections of his life in Edinburgh with the Fairfords, and with his memories, dim as they are, of his own family. Darsie explains his motives for recalling his past near the close of the letter:

> I repeat the little history now, as I have a hundred times before, merely because I would wring some sense out of it. Turn, then, thy sharp, wire-drawing, lawyer-like ingenuity to this same task − make up my history as though thou wert shaping the blundering allegations of some blue-bonneted, hard-headed client into a condescendence of facts and circumstances, and thou shalt be, not my Apollo, − *quid tibi cum lyra* − but my Lord Stair.   (Letter 1; 11)

The tone of the letter is playful, even mocking, as if these matters were no real burden to Darsie, or, by implication, to his creator. But Darsie's teasing has a serious purpose. In proposing that Alan employ his lawyerly skills, Darsie is asking his friend to "make up" a history for him, to place his memories into some semblance of order. Darsie's letter is a plea for interpretation. But in *Redgauntlet* interpretation is not merely a sorting-out process, a matter of discovering the deeper coherence in a collection of seemingly disparate events. It is a process of shaping mere "blundering allegations" into a persuasive "case."

The case of Peter Peebles vs. Paul Plainstanes is Scott's most explicit linkage between the figures of the lawyer and the taleteller. Peebles's own remarks about his case point to its typicality: "It is like a specimen of all causes, man. By the Regiam, there is not a *remedium juris* in the practiques but ye'll find a spice o't" (Letter 13; 231). Saunders Fairford views Peebles vs. Plainstanes as a source of exercise for his son's legal skills, comparing it to the cadaver on which a surgeon's apprentice hones his talents in practice for working on a live patient (Letter 13; 220). It is a hopeless cause, the despair of many a bright young newcomer to the Outer House, an insoluble legal riddle made up of suit upon countersuit. Alan describes the case to Darsie as "lawsuit within lawsuit," resembling a "nest of chip-boxes" (Letter 13; 229), which he is somehow supposed to extricate one from the other. But in Alan's capable hands, Peebles vs. Plainstanes takes on a coherence before the court which it had hitherto lacked. Alan presents Peter Peebles as a sympathetic character, a man consistently and repeatedly cheated of his rightful claims by the subtle machinations of a corrupt partner. He exhibits his client to the judgment of the court as the unfortunate and undeserving victim of his business associate, and of the legal system itself, which has permitted and even encouraged the success of "well-invented but unfounded counter-claims ..." (ch. 1; 251).

Alan acquits himself brilliantly, laying "before the court a clear and intelligible statement of the affairs of the copartnery," sorting out the accounts of the partnership, and in the process, placing the "artful interpolations and insertions of the fallacious Plainstanes against each other and against the fact" (ch. 1; 250–51). The court appears convinced by Alan's discourse of the justice of Mr. Peebles's longstanding claim. But the opposing counsel raises an objection to Alan's statement of the case, noting a point his colleague has neglected which is "founded on the interpretation of certain correspondence which had passed betwixt the parties soon after the dissolution of the copartnery" (ch. 1; 253). While this is perhaps merely a stratagem by opposing counsel to diminish the force of Alan's reasoning on the decision of the judges, this "point," founded only on "interpretation," becomes yet another obstacle to the successful issue of Peebles's suit. A problem of interpretation, possibly invented, thus renders the case of Peebles vs. Plainstanes, which had been so carefully sorted out through the exertions of Alan and his father, a legal enigma once again, subject to yet another effort of interpretation.

Scott even suggests that the court is concerned primarily not with establishing the facts of the case, but with the quality of the young lawyer's performance. The advocate's own statement is rife with "artful interpolations":

"Their association," said Alan, and the little flight was received with some applause, "resembled the ancient story of the fruit which was carved with a knife poisoned on one side of the blade only, so that the individual to whom the envenomed portion was served drew decay and death from what afforded savour and sustenance to the consumer of the other moiety." (ch. 1; 250)

Alan's simile, used to illustrate the essential features of Peebles's relationship with Plainstanes, draws the applause of the court, as if his presentation were as much a theatrical performance as a legal disquisition. Alan has claimed in his argument that Plainstanes, in preying upon his former benefactor, has invented stories about the partnership to conceal his crimes. But Alan's version of the case, Scott is clearly suggesting here, is founded, at least in part, on invention. In defending his client, Alan sets "just claims" against "well-invented but unfounded counterclaims," the facts of the case against the compelling fictions of Plainstanes and his lawyers. But Scott's treatment of the case endorses neither fact nor fiction, but rather sets fictions beside one another and judges them as artistic gestures. Alan's argument to the judges is not primarily a statement of fact, but a kind of audition-piece for which the cause of Peter Peebles serves as a pretext.

As Darsie's advocate, Alan must assemble a history for his client. The task of making up the case requires the establishment of Darsie's paternal origins, the tracing of a genealogy. Alan's warnings to Darsie in the early letters reflect his emphasis on the real social world, where the accurate evaluation of human character is an essential skill, where one must be sure of one's self and the individual to whom one is talking, and avoid making up stories which might distort the facts. His admonitions to Darsie against the untrammeled exercise of his imagination contain one of the novel's central ideological motives. The point of Alan's efforts to keep his friend's feet on the ground is to socialize Darsie Latimer, to make him a part of that real world in which character is fixed, in which the qualities of good and bad are determinate, and discernible to the disciplined judgment of a mature observer. Darsie's plea to Alan in his first letter is not only a plea for interpretation, but for assimilation as well. Making up a history for Darsie Latimer means establishing his social identity, placing him within a particular pattern of family relations. For Scott, that means the writing of a genealogical fiction. Making up Darsie's case means writing a family history.

The elevation of status Scott manages for Darsie repeats the familiar pattern of the Waverley endings, but with an important variation. Scott's concern with discovering the familial identity of his protagonist links the novel with *The Heart of Midlothian*. In Scott's reflections on the Union, the Deanses and the Stauntons represent the family of Britain. Effie Deans's sin of fornication is not only a crime against the institution of marriage, but a flouting of the greater social hierarchy. The affair of Effie and Staunton is emblematic of the degraded condition of the Scottish nation and of the Kingdom as a whole. The fabric of British society has been rent by revolt. Fathers and sons are estranged from one another. A scion of the English aristocracy turns rebel and debases himself among the lower orders, inciting the Edinburgh mob to riot. Children defy their parents, and Scotland threatens to rebel against England.

In obtaining a pardon for her sister, Jeanie Deans seeks at once to clear Effie of the charge of infanticide and to bring her back within the fold of the family. The closing chapters of *Midlothian* represent an effort to restore the integrity of the family, and, by implication, the greater political entity of the Kingdom. Scott's pastoral was written to undo the awful work of history and to serve as a fable of national regeneration. The history Darsie Latimer asks his friend to "make up" for him is a fable of identity. Scott's narrative brings the hero the knowledge for which he has long yearned, and in the process, raises him from the status of affluent orphanhood to the head of an ancient estate, thereby guaranteeing perpetuity to an illustrious family threatened with extinction by the forces of history.

If the seemingly real world of lawyers and judges to which Alan belongs is contaminated by fiction, then the distinction between romance and reality is useful only as a means of generic description. The practice of law comes to resemble the practice of taletelling, and Alan Fairford becomes, like Darsie Latimer, a figure of imagination. Scott's novelistic practice reproduces the methods of the young lawyer. Alan takes in hand the disparate pieces of Peebles' cause, suit and countersuit, and makes out of them a story calculated to elicit the sympathy of his audience, and thereby to carry his client's claim. Scott uses facts drawn from previous accounts of British history, individuals, events, geographical settings, and arranges them in the form of a compelling story about the past, a story which expresses and endorses a particular ideological bias, a political claim about the meaning of history.

Behind the letters of Darsie and Alan is the implication that the worlds defined in the dialogue, the realm of romance and the realm of things as they are, are both imaginative constructs. But while Scott acknowledges his own "artful interpolations" in handling the case he calls *Redgauntlet*, he does not settle easily into a position of relativism. Into the contest of opposing visions established in the opening pages, he inserts what appears to be a mediating figure, the Quaker Joshua Geddes. F. R. Hart has described Geddes as an "ideal speaker, for whom speech is to convey the truth, yet keep the peace."[5] Geddes appears initially to represent plain speech, the ideal of a natural language against the artificial languages spoken by the novel's principal characters. He seems, as Hart aptly expresses it, "anti-romance personified,"[6] the idea of a transparent language cast in the form of Darsie Latimer's friend and protector. He proves a true friend to Darsie, kindhearted and loyal, willing to put himself in danger in order to rescue Darsie from the hands of the Laird. But Geddes is a more complicated figure than Hart's theory would allow. The Quaker has derived his surname from an old family of Jacobite loyalties which had, until recent times, engaged wholeheartedly in the political adventures of the Stuart party. His ancestors, Geddes informs his guest, had accrued their wealth and made their reputation by "freebooting, robbery, and bloodshed," and so had acquired the name "Geddes," "the shark of the fresh waters" (Letter 7; 104). The Quaker's recounting of his family's chequered past is occasioned by Darsie's remarks on noticing the defacement of an armorial scutcheon on the front of the parlour chimney: "The hammer, or chisel, which had been employed to deface the shield and crest had left uninjured the scroll beneath, which bore the pious motto, 'Trust in God'." The present inhabitant of the house has thus preserved only the virtuous motto of the family crest. With his passion for deciphering "black-letter," Darsie reads this fragmented symbol of the "forgotten dead," and repeats the motto to his host. His expression of sorrow at the defacement of the scutcheon elicits from Geddes an account of the family since the "benighted" times of Papistry. Joshua's disclaimer of vanity with regard to his ancient pedigree is belied by "the air of mingled melancholy, regret, and conscious dignity" with which he tells the story. There is an element of pride even in his disavowal, suggesting a lingering attachment to the family's past, a need to recall his origins even as he condemns his ancestors as "ravenous and bloodthirsty" (Letter 7; 103–4).

Having acquired a modest fortune through commercial ventures, Phillip Geddes, Joshua's father, was able to redeem a portion of the property which his forebears had called Sharingknowe. In restoring the family estate, Phillip, himself a Quaker, had changed its name "in sense, without much alteration of sound" (Letter 7; 107), calling it Mount Sharon, with no pun intended. Phillip not only altered the name of the place, but destroyed most of the remnants of the old house, and built in its stead a modern mansion, preserving the old hearth and pious motto, and obliterating the secular and martial emblems of the scutcheon. What Joshua's father accomplished in these acts was no less than a rewriting of his family's history. Phillip's gestures were at once redemptive and destructive. Like Peter Pattieson, the fictional editor of Old Mortality's anecdotes, he has rechiselled the inscriptions made by his predecessors. While Old Mortality had sought to revive the memory of the Whig martyrs by renewing the inscriptions on their tombstones, Phillip Geddes attempted to obviate the symbols of the "forgotten dead," to cancel out the bad and preserve the good. The defacement of the armorial scutcheon and the alteration of the property's name are denials of the family's past, distortions of history which express the prejudices of the modern Geddeses and which allow them at the same time to preserve some remnants of the old estate.

Scott's pun on "Sharingknowe" in the evangelical appellation of "Mount Sharon" is a trick played against the Quaker, a quiet way of undermining Joshua's credibility on the issue of linguistic precision. After hearing Darsie's account of his night at the Laird's, Joshua expresses some doubt as to its veracity. To Darsie's reply that such a deception would be without motive or object, the Quaker responds by observing his own people's fidelity to the truth in their use of language, against the habitual mendacity of Darsie's: "... Thou knowest that thine own people do not, as we humbly endeavour to do, confine themselves within the simplicity of truth, but employ the language of falsehood, not only for profit, but for compliment, and sometimes for mere diversion" (Letter 6; 89). Yet there is no lack of art at Mount Sharon. Despite Joshua's solemn claims to truthful expression, the estate itself is obviously a product of artifice. In contrast to the relative simplicity of the house, the gardens and offices "might rival an earl's in point of care and expense" (Letter 7; 111). Darsie's expressions of admiration for the elaborate design of the garden suggest that the plainness and simplicity which Joshua claims for his language is merely a style, a manner of speaking rather than a natural language:

There were various compartments, the connection of which was well managed, and although the whole ground did not exceed five or six acres, it was so varied as to seem four times larger. The space contained close alleys and open walks; a very pretty artificial waterfall, a fountain also, consisting of a considerable jet d'eau, whose stream glittered in the sunbeams and exhibited a continual rainbow ... I know that you, Alan, will condemn all this as bad and antiquated; for ever since Dodsley has described the Leasowes and talked of Brown's imitations of nature, and Horace Walpole's late Essay on Gardening, you are all for simple nature − condemn walking up and down stairs in the open air and declare for wood and wilderness.   (Letter 7; 113)

But Scott's purpose here is not simply to illustrate the vanity behind the plain speech of the Quaker. The art of Mount Sharon has an effect beyond the deception of the senses; it involves more than the use of the picturesque for the sake of decoration. Darsie complains that there is no imaginative literature in the library of the Quaker's house, only a collection of religious and moral tracts and a few volumes of historical writing for the edification of the inhabitants and their guests. But art rules, even in a world seemingly hostile to the faculty of fancy which Darsie so prizes. The illusions created by the landscape architect form an image of "good order" (Letter 7; 112), serving as a shelter against the rough and inhospitable prospect of the Dumfriesshire downs. Mount Sharon stands as an illusion of peace and harmony in a Border region where conflict is the rule.

Finding the quiet round of life at Mount Sharon "insipid," longing for "stream and cataract," Darsie leaves Geddes's "cultivated farm and ornamented grounds" behind him, as if he were escaping "from the realms of art into those of free and unconstrained nature" (Letter 10; 146–47). On his excursion into the links of Dumfriesshire, Darsie stumbles into the company of Blind Willie Ste'enson, a musician and taleteller of local renown, who regales the traveler with a supernatural story, a narrative of the taleteller's own ancestral past. His wandering thus leads him not from art to nature, but from art to art, from one generic realm into another, by way of nature, from the mingling of plain style with picturesque at Mount Sharon into the mixed mode of Wandering Willie's vision. Set off from the main body of Darsie's letter, "Wandering Willie's Tale" is marked by Scott as a story within a story. Willie's account of a visit to hell follows an old folk tradition with which Scott, as a collector of ballads and legends, was undoubtedly familiar.[7] Beyond its entertainment value as a ghost story and its dubious merit as a register of lower-class consciousness, the tale serves Scott as a medium for reflecting on the technique of the novel. Reading beneath the supernatural plot, Avrom Fleishman regards the story as "a folk parable of the Redgauntlets' splendid past, their decline in fortune (till it plumbs bottom at a revel of the devil and his assorted Jacobite followers), and their comic defeat by a crafty peasant."[8] The tale is presented in such a way that the historical interpretation favored by Fleishman appears highly plausible. But the reader is required neither to accept the tale at face value nor to perform the particular kind of allegorical reduction which makes of the tale a cleverly coded account of a crucial period in Scottish history.

"Wandering Willie's Tale" repeats in more elaborate form Scott's exploitation of the supernatural in *The Bride of Lammermoor*. In *The Bride*, Scott holds out two distinct interpretative possibilities, the supernatural and the rational, and appears to come down decisively on the side of the rational. Like the reader of "Wandering Willie's Tale," Edgar Ravenswood is faced with the dilemma of how to understand the course of events which had led up to his courtship of Lucy Ashton. While Scott firmly rejects the perceptions of " 'the superstitious eye'," he allows the supernatural perspective to stand as a historically determined way of seeing, a mode of vision once dominant, but which, with the gradual movement of history, has become obsolete. As narrator of the "Tale," Willie suggests rational explanations for the strange events which he relates, but also hints that the plot may be literally true, that his grandfather may, in fact, have actually visited hell to retrieve a rent receipt. In acknowledging that the jackanapes which Sir Robert kept as a pet might well have caused much of the mischief, Willie implies that perhaps there is, after all, a simple, realistic way of accounting for his grandfather's recovery of the receipt. Yet at the close of the tale, Willie announces that "the truth," which only "Heaven kens," "first came out by the minister's wife," and that his grandfather was then "obliged to tell the real narrative to his friends, for the credit of his good name" (Letter 11; 192). Willie's language is designed to allow for multiple interpretations, to invite the imaginative reader to concoct one of his own. The "real narrative" is "Wandering Willie's Tale" itself, a fact which would seem to do the teller "credit" only by enhancing his reputation as a taleteller.[9]

The telling of the story and its transmission from generation to generation serves the same larger purpose as Darsie's recounting of his adventures to his friend. Willie's "Tale" is at once a genealogical and a historical fiction. In telling the "Tale," Willie not only sketches out an episode of family history, but restores the "credit" of Steenie's and Willie's "good name" by distinguishing servant from master, by passing judgment, moral and historical, on the Redgauntlet family. In the "Tale," Steenie is a gifted musician, an artist, easygoing and hapless, who has become implicated by his master in the oppression of Covenanters: "He saw muckle mischief and maybe did some, that he couldna avoid" (Letter 11; 167). Although Steenie was no party man himself, neither Whig nor Jacobite, the placing of his master in hell represents a clear moral verdict against Robert Redgauntlet and his cohorts. But while the company of cavaliers is condemned by the moral vision of the "Tale," the past which is embodied in the figure of Sir Robert Redgauntlet retains a certain appeal. Sir Robert's values are both rejected and sanctioned by the narrative. The hell to which Steenie pays his call is an underworld version of the family mansion. There is little suffering here. The place seems, indeed, to have about it a festive atmosphere, and Steenie is invited to partake, as in old times, in the raucous conviviality of Sir Robert and his cavalier comrades. Even in the depths of hell, the master of the estate remains loyal to his servant. Steenie does, after all, get his receipt from Sir Robert.

The "Tale" contains, in small, the key formal and thematic patterns of *Redgauntlet*. Its place within the correspondence is worth considering. Material which Scott has elsewhere inserted in a framing chapter is placed between the lines of a personal letter. Willie tells the tale to Darsie just as Darsie relates his adventures to Alan, and as Alan, in turn, exchanges his own adventures with Darsie. In one sense, at least, the "Tale" is a story of familial origins, in which Willie describes the pattern of his ancestry and places his family in relation to the noble family of Redgauntlet, which has played a central rôle in Scottish history. As a historical work, the "Tale" represents, as Fleishman perceived, Scott's preferred version of the past.

Within the structure of the narrative, the problems of interpretation Scott thematizes in *Redgauntlet*, and throughout the Waverley novels, are raised and left only partially resolved. By setting the "Tale" apart from the main body of the novel, Scott emphasizes its status as a story about the past. He uses the "Tale" not only as a parable of the Redgauntlets' past, but as a parable of the novel itself.

Situated as it is, Willie's tale becomes another layer of narrative within Darsie's account of his experience and another version of Darsie's attempt to render his own past in the form of a history. But the "Tale" is also the first source for Darsie, and for the reader as well, of the story of Sir Alberic Redgauntlet. It is at once a source of information about Darsie's familial past and of interpretations of that past. The turn which Scott makes with Willie's tale is implied in its dual status as a story of the past and as a source of knowledge. In *Redgauntlet*, the past is available only through twice-told tales. The narrator's account of things is true only to the degree that we accept the truth of his story.

In the closing chapters of *Old Mortality*, Scott's narrator asserts the prerogative of the taleteller to ignore the dramatic unities and to rearrange the course of events as he pleases, to make things up as he wishes without observing the conventions of plausibility. This prerogative is assumed in *Redgauntlet*. But now Scott asserts the power of the taleteller by placing one within the main part of the novel. The figure of Blind Willie Ste'enson serves Scott as both an artist and a narrator. Like his grandfather, Willie is detached from political conflict, from the struggles described in the "Tale" and in the novel. Although he will be implicated in Hugh Redgauntlet's scheme of rebellion, his devotion to the family is personal rather than political in character. He serves Darsie and Darsie's uncle as well, without prejudice for either beyond his loyalty to the family. In this feature, there is an important parallel between Darsie and Blind Willie. While Darsie finally takes sides at the prospect of participating in his uncle's rebellion, through much of the novel he is a non-partisan figure, in both a political and literary sense. Given to writing romantic histories of himself, Darsie nonetheless seeks from his pragmatic and realistic counterpart in the epistolary dialogue a rational explanation of his parentage. Committed provisionally to the mode of romance, he asks Alan to help him find his place in the world of "real history." In assuming the title of Sir Arthur Darsie Redgauntlet, he acquires the social identity of heir to an old landed family, and so finds his place in the "real" world. Darsie has rejected the pattern of self-destructive violence in which his uncle had participated and eschewed his uncle's belief in a mysterious Necessity which determines the destiny of the family. Yet despite his refusal to share the vision of his uncle, Darsie's career in the novel is itself a form of "romantic history."

Among the artist-figures of the novel, Scott's closest counterpart is Hugh Redgauntlet. Redgauntlet is a character of nearly Protean powers, making himself over as the situation demands, appearing variously as the Laird, as Herries of Birrenswork, and as Squire Ingoldsby. He makes himself Darsie's guardian before a magistrate, even though he can prove no familial connection at the moment. He tears up the King's writ, as if it were merely a legal fabrication, and consigns it to the fire. In the letters of Darsie and Alan, he acquires a supernatural dimension, seeming to appear at once in Solway, Edinburgh, and Cumberland, spearing salmon on the Firth, inciting the local fishermen to riot against the fishnets, calling on Saunders Fairford in the person of an elderly gentleman of reduced fortunes, exploiting and then defying the authority of a magistrate.

Redgauntlet's ambition is to reverse the historical developments of half a century, to transform the course of British history just as he has transformed himself. But his strategies are finally undermined by the changes which have occurred gradually in the two decades since the last Jacobite uprising. When the moment for action arrives, Redgauntlet's seemingly magical powers fail him. He has succeeded in bringing together the most prominent Jacobites in the country with the Stuart heir. But Bonnie Prince Charlie, with his mistress in tow, is no longer quite so "bonnie" in the view of his old sympathizers. In his reactionary fervor, Hugh Redgauntlet has failed to recognize the signs of a subtle, but significant, alteration in the minds of his former comrades-in-arms. Forced to accompany his uncle to the assembly at Crackenthorp's public house, Darsie discovers little enthusiasm for revolution in the company of the rebels: "... he thought he could discern in it few traces of that adventurous hope which urges men upon desperate enterprises; and began to believe that the conspiracy would dissolve of itself ..." But Hugh Redgauntlet, either out of blindness, or out of a willful refusal to see things as they are, exhorts the company to do battle once more against the forces of the usurper: "Mr. Redgauntlet ... did not, or would not, see any such marks of depression of spirit amongst his coadjutors, but met them with cheerful countenance and a warm greeting of welcome." Oblivious to the "ominous melancholy" which marks their formal salutes, he attempts to rouse their martial spirit, recalling old battles and hinting at future victories (ch. 22; 313–14). But all his conjuring cannot incite the assemblage to rebellion. History is against the Jacobite party, despite the unpopularity of the current regime; and history, as Scott has so often demonstrated, will have its way.

But while the artistry of Hugh Redgauntlet is finally thwarted, another Redgauntlet survives the novel's crisis on the winning side. Having experienced the world of romance, Darsie returns, shed of his romantic dreams, to the "real" world from which he had set out. The pattern of Darsie's career serves a double purpose for Scott. In submitting his character to the realm of romance and then bringing him back to the novelistic world, Scott at once rejects and ratifies the power of romance. The gesture which brings Darsie, quite literally, into the hands of his uncle, is the rescue on the sands of Solway. The rescue acquires a complicated meaning later in the novel, once the reader has learned the story of Sir Alberic Redgauntlet and his son and discovered that Darsie is the lost heir to the Redgauntlet title. But this significance is beyond the immediate comprehension of the correspondents. Darsie's imaginative extravagance makes of the rescue an event of great portent, while Alan's common sense reduces the image of "Atlantes on his hippogriff" to the figure of "some high-kilted fishwife" carrying a truant schoolboy home from a careless wade in the Leith (Letter 5; 65–66). Placed within the larger context of the Redgauntlet family history and the political struggles with which that history is intertwined, the rescue becomes a reversal of that fateful encounter in which Alberic Redgauntlet murdered his own son.

The Redgauntlets are doomed to political failure because Alberic, placing patriotic duty above the bonds of family, trampled his own son to death in pursuit of an enemy. But Hugh Redgauntlet saves his nephew, who proves an opponent of his cause, once inadvertently, and a second time in full awareness of the young man's identity and political position. The central romantic character of the novel, who confirms the presence of the tell-tale pattern in Darsie's brow ("the fatal mark of our race"), who professes his unshakeable belief in a great "web of destiny by which we are all surrounded" (ch. 8; 28–36), is thus instrumental in the ultimate reversal of the family's fortunes. Redgauntlet's actions violate the very pattern of fatality he traces in his nephew's countenance. The rescue of Darsie and his eventual restoration to his patrimony reverse the filicidal gesture which has long reverberated through the family history, and lead to the destruction of his uncle's dream of rebellion.

But Darsie's career confirms another kind of fatality, endorsing the very values it subverts. The novel's extremely brief "Conclusion" completes the triumph of common sense which had begun with the arrival of General Campbell and the peaceful dispersal of the Jacobite assemblage. Yet in these same gestures Scott brings to fruition the "romantic history" of Darsie Latimer which Alan had described in an effort to discourage his friend's flights of imagination:

> But what dost thou look to? The chance that the mystery, as you call it, which at present overclouds your birth and connexions will clear up into something inexpressibly and inconceivably brilliant; and this without any effort or exertion of your own, but purely by the good-will of Fortune.
>
> (Letter 2; 25)

Scott's endorsement of this romantic self-conception implies his acceptance of romance not only as a way of perceiving, but of reconstructing history as well. What Scott shares with Hugh Redgauntlet is not a belief in the force of "destiny," but a confidence in the revisionary powers of his own fictions. In the process of composing his novels, Scott performs a series of self-transformations. In *Redgauntlet*, he speaks first in the voice of Darsie Latimer, then of Alan Fairford, and then in the voice of omniscient narration. Working in his various disguises, Scott attempts to recast history, to recreate the past as he wished it had happened. The artist-figures of the novel are metafictional instruments for the author, fashioned from the models of earlier works. Through these characters, Scott comments on the art of writing history as he practices it, asserting the prerogatives of the taleteller as he presents his own stories of the past. The feature which unifies the disparate stories given in *Redgauntlet* is the figure of the taleteller, the character who both observes the past and presents it in accordance with the contours of his own vision.[10]

The formal and ideological tensions of the early novels clearly carry over into *Redgauntlet*. But while the modal mixture of the earlier work persists, in the later novel, modal mixture has become the central subject of Scott's writing. In *Waverley* and *Old Mortality*, Scott was deeply concerned with representing the truth of history. Keenly aware of his own reliance on romance as a means of rewriting history, Scott nevertheless aspired to the accurate depiction of things as they were.

If his novels could not record the actuality of the past, they could at least approximate the effect of histories, and thereby serve a more serious purpose than mere romances. But in *Redgauntlet* Scott has set aside his ambition to write a faithful account of the past, and composed a piece of self-reflexive romance about writing history. For the Scott of *Redgauntlet*, the preferred mode of writing history is romance. Knowing that romance distorts history, Scott exploits that power of distortion in drawing his pictures of the past.

NOTES

1 THE HISTORICAL NOVEL AND THE PRODUCTION OF THE PAST

1 See James T. Hillhouse, *The Waverley Novels and Their Critics* (Minneapolis: University of Minnesota Press, 1936), pp. 42–47. Hillhouse's survey indicates that the focus on historical authenticity has a precedent in the reviews of Scott's contemporaries. See especially Hillhouse's discussion of Francis Jeffrey's remarks in the *Edinburgh Review*. For contemporary instances of the historical emphasis, see James Anderson, *Sir Walter Scott and History* (Edinburgh: Oliver & Boyd, 1981); David Brown, *Walter Scott and the Historical Imagination* (London: Routledge & Kegan Paul, 1979); A. O. J. Cockshut, *The Achievement of Walter Scott* (London: Collins, 1969); David Daiches, "Scott's Achievement as a Novelist," *Nineteenth-Century Fiction*, 6 (September 1951), pp. 80–95, and (December 1951), pp. 153–73; and D. D. Devlin, *The Author of Waverley* (London: Macmillan, 1971). The best work of the sixties after Lukács, Alexander Welsh's *The Hero of the Waverley Novels* (New Haven and London: Yale University Press, 1963), emphasized the romance elements of Scott's fiction over the historical. Treating the novels as "projective romances," Welsh defined the ideological preconditions of Scott's writing, placing the historical romancer among such figures as Burke and Gladstone as a kindred mind. For the best recent studies of Scott, see George Levine's appraisal in *The Realistic Imagination: English Fiction from Frankenstein to Lady Chatterley* (Chicago: University of Chicago Press, 1981), pp. 81–128. Levine treats Scott as a lighthearted artificer rather than an earnest depictor of the past, a figure who manipulates literary conventions in the service of a Whig historical vision. See also Harry E. Shaw, *The Forms of Historical Fiction: Sir Walter Scott and His Successors* (Ithaca: Cornell University Press, 1983); Jane Millgate, *Walter Scott: The Making of the Novelist* (Toronto: University of Toronto Press, 1984); Daniel Cottom, *The Civilized Imagination: A Study of Ann Radcliffe, Jane Austen, and Sir Walter Scott* (Cambridge: Cambridge

University Press, 1985), pp. 127–92; Judith Wilt, *Secret Leaves: The Novels of Sir Walter Scott* (Chicago: University of Chicago Press, 1985). Wilt offers the most comprehensive and theoretically elaborate treatment yet published of Scott's novelistic imagination, and a compelling argument for Scott as a major English novelist in the line of Dickens, George Eliot, and Thackeray.

2 See Georg Lukács, *The Historical Novel*, trans. Hannah and Stanley Mitchell (Lincoln and London: University of Nebraska Press), p. 32. Lukács credits Scott with presenting the "'middle way,'" the famous English compromise which is the truth of the nation's history: "He attempts by fathoming historically the whole of English development to find a 'middle way' for himself between the warring extremes. He finds in English history the consolation that the most violent vicissitudes of class struggle have always finally calmed down into a glorious 'middle way'."

3 Terry Eagleton, *Criticism and Ideology: A Study in Marxist Literary Theory* (London: Verso, 1980), p. 70.

4 Eagleton, *Criticism and Ideology*, pp. 74–75.

5 As I use the word here, "ideology" refers to a set of discourses, values, and representations, relatively unified and logically consistent, which reflect the experiential relations of individuals to their social conditions in such a way as to ensure misapprehension of the real.

6 Eagleton, *Criticism and Ideology*, p. 72.

7 See Michael Hechter, *Internal Colonialism: The Celtic Fringe in British National Development* (Berkeley and Los Angeles: University of California Press, 1975), p. 32. For a broad description of the relations between the British "core" and the Celtic "periphery," see pp. 39ff. Hechter regards the Scottish Highlands as a part of the Celtic "periphery" conquered by Britain in the eighteenth century. The relationship between Britain and the Highlands, Wales, and Ireland was a "colonial situation," in which the dominated territories were condemned to an instrumental role with respect to the British "metropolis." According to Hechter, the "internal campaigns" against the Celtic fringe "were not coincidental to overseas colonization, but the result of the same social forces within Great Britain ..."

8 Cf. Judith Wilt, *Secret Leaves*, p. 19. Wilt borrows the motif of "kidnapped romance" from Frye's *The Secular Scripture* to argue for the centrality of Scott's fiction, particularly *Waverley* and *Ivanhoe*: "... Frye's claim that Romance is the fundamental condition of storytelling, related to all further modes (realism) or genres (the realistic novel) not by replacement or even transformation but rather by kidnapping, seems utterly appropriate to *Waverley*, which is as artifact, who is, as character, the very type of kidnapped romance."

9 Hayden White, "The Historical Text as Literary Artifact," in R. Canary and H. Kozicki, eds., *The Writing of History: Literary Form and Historical Understanding* (Madison: University of Wisconsin Press, 1978), pp. 42, 50–51. See also Louis O. Mink, "History and Fiction as Modes of Comprehension," in *New Directions in Literary History*, ed. Ralph Cohen (Baltimore: Johns Hopkins University Press, 1974), p. 117. Mink finds in both history and fiction a common commitment to "story" as a form of explanation and to a larger "configurational" frame of perception. In the "configurational" mode defined by Mink, things are comprehended "as elements in a single and concrete complex of relationships." Things belong "to a particular configuration of events, like a part to a jigsaw puzzle. It is in this *configurational* mode that we see together the complex of imagery in a poem or the combination of motives, pressures, promises and principles which explain a Senator's voice, or the pattern of words, gestures, and actions which constitute our understanding of the personality of a friend."

10 Sir Walter Scott, *Waverley: Or 'tis Sixty Years Since* (Edinburgh: T. and A. Constable, 1901–03), pp. 10–11. All references to Scott's novels are to this edition (see my "Note on citations of the Waverley novels," p. ix). Subsequent references to them will be given by division (chapter or letter) and page number in the main text.

11 Sir Walter Scott, "Introduction" to *The Castle of Otranto*, ed. Caroline Spurgeon (New York: Macmillan, 1947), pp. xxxiii–xxxiv.

12 Scott, "Introduction" to *The Castle of Otranto*, pp. xxxvii–xl.

13 "Introduction" to *The Castle of Otranto*, p. xl.

14 See David Punter, *The Literature of Terror: A History of Gothic Fiction from 1765 to the Present* (London: Longman, 1980), p. 163.

15 Tzvetan Todorov, *The Fantastic: A Structural Approach to a Literary Genre* (Ithaca: Cornell University Press, 1975), p. 25.

16 Todorov, *The Fantastic*, p. 25.

17 See David Daiches, "Scott's Achievement as a Novelist," *Nineteenth Century Fiction*, 6 (September 1951), pp. 80–95 and (December 1951), pp. 153–73, rpt. in A. Norman Jeffares, ed., *Scott's Mind and Art* (New York: Barnes and Noble), p. 24.

18 See Edgar Johnson, *Sir Walter Scott: The Great Unknown* (New York: Macmillan, 1970), p. 586. Johnson cites a letter from Scott to John Ballantyne of October 1817 from H. J. C. Grierson, *The Letters of Sir Walter Scott* (Oxford: Oxford University Press, 1932–37), vol. 5, p. 5: "I have closed with Usher for his beautiful patrimony, which makes me a great laird. I am afraid the people will take me up for coining. Indeed these novels, while their attractions last, are something like it …"

19 See Fredric Jameson, *The Political Unconscious: Narrative as a Socially*

Symbolic Act (Ithaca: Cornell University Press, 1981), p.48. Writing of Balzac's *La Vieille Fille*, Fredric Jameson uses "political fantasy" to describe "the mapping of that particular 'libidinal apparatus' in which Balzac's political thinking becomes invested ... [a] protonarrative structure ... [which is] the vehicle for our experience of the real." I use "political fantasy" with some license here, as a sort of intermediate term, suggesting not an illusion projected onto reality by the novelist, but the form in and through which history is retextualized in fiction. While the term could thus also designate ideology, "fantasy" carries with it a psychoanalytic connotation: it is the form of a wish emanating from the political unconscious.

20 Johnson, *Sir Walter Scott: The Great Unknown*, p.108.

21 See W. E. K. Anderson, ed., *The Journal of Sir Walter Scott* (London: Oxford University Press, 1972), p.43.

22 See Harry E. Shaw, *The Forms of Historical Fiction*, pp.214–26. Shaw's discussion of *The Bride* as a reworking of this traumatic episode in Scott's personal history is a brilliant exception.

23 Shaw, *The Forms of Historical Fiction*, p.216.

24 See Welsh, *The Hero of the Waverley Novels*, p.122: "Property, conceived as 'sluggish, inert and timid,' and entirely defensive in power is the best key we have to the inactivity of the hero in the Waverley novels ..." Those who fail to respect "Property," be they "romantic principals" or landgrabbing *arriviste* types, are typically exiled or snuffed out.

25 See *The Works of the Right Honourable Edmund Burke* (London: Oxford University Press, 1907), vol.4, pp.55–56. Scott's attitude toward the idea of property, insofar as he can be said to have consciously held one, bears a near resemblance to the notion elaborated by Edmund Burke in his *Reflections on the Revolution in France*. For the Burke of *Reflections*, property is both a conventional and a natural relation. The principle of poverty is derived from the pattern of nature and applied artificially to create a workable order in society: "The possessors of family wealth, and of the distinction which attends hereditary possession (as most concerned with it) are the natural securities for this transmission." Preserved within the enduring social structure of the ancient landed families, property and, therefore, political power are transmitted in orderly fashion from generation to generation.

26 F. A. Pottle, "The Power of Memory in Boswell and Scott," in A. Norman Jeffares, ed., *Scott's Mind and Art* (New York: Barnes and Noble, 1970), pp.230–53.

27 Pottle, "The Power of Memory in Boswell and Scott," pp.236–37.

2 THE REEMPLOTMENT OF REBELLION:
WAVERLEY AND *OLD MORTALITY*

1 See Welsh, *The Hero of the Waverley Novels*, pp. 147–48: "The romance, of course, is not over. By 'romance,' Waverley means the romantic episode, which, we have observed, is characteristically finite. By 'history,' he signifies an equally imaginary construction of infinite future time – a part of the reality by which the hero conceives himself to be supported. "

2 For readings of *Waverley* as a *Bildungsroman*, see S. Stewart Gordon, "*Waverley* and the Unified Design," *ELH*, 18 (1957), pp. 107–22, and F. R. Hart, *Scott's Novels: The Plotting of Historic Survival* (Charlottesville: University of Virginia Press, 1966), pp. 14–31. See Shaw, *The Forms of Historical Fiction*, pp. 179–80, for a persuasive argument against the *Bildungsroman* reading. Shaw points to Waverley's rescue of Colonel Talbot from the Jacobite troops as an instance of one possible turning point. "A Bildungsroman reading of the novel naturally wants to consider this a moment of decisive moral growth."

3 See Levine, *The Realistic Imagination*, pp. 82, 88: "[Scott] was only making things up for the entertainment of his audience, and the tricks he played on them, the disguises, the self-reflexive games he intruded into the novels, were essentially honest revelations of the fictionality of the fictions." Speaking of *Waverley*'s artificial ending, Levine observes that Scott's unabashed trickery serves the author's conception of history: "As the tricks reemerge from the romancer's bag ... they begin to do the work of history itself. The tag, 'They lived happily ever after,' in Scott is likely to mean that the protagonist, having found the right side in large historical conflicts, is rewarded personally with the success of the winning party. The good fortune which befalls the hero is absurd in particular but truthful in general."

I am also indebted to P. D. Garside, "*Waverley*'s Pictures of the Past," *ELH*, 44 (1977), pp. 660, 664. According to Garside, the numerous "pictures of the past" presented in *Waverley*, including gazette reports, family legends, paintings, letters, depictions of landscape, parallel the processes of "historical reportage generally." Scott writes in *Waverley* with the insight that "presentation" lends to events a dignity or even majesty inherently lacking in them. For Scott, Garside argues, "presentation" is inevitably a "process of gradual distortion" accomplished through "a series of distances." See also Joseph Valente, "Upon the Braes: History and Hermeneutics in *Waverley*," *Studies in Romanticism*, 25 (Summer 1986), pp. 251–76: "History is not a given in *Waverley*. Defined by opposition to the concept of romance, history is a problem, a problem with roots in epistemology and hermeneutics. Indeed, the topos of history and romance in *Waverley* serves precisely to thematize the fundamentally interpretive dimension of human experience.''

4 See Levine, *The Realistic Imagination*, pp. 104–05: ''The great historical experience just narrated becomes in the text itself a work of art, distanced and romantic, yet realistic. History is thus aestheticized. The fact is there, but the practical force of the fact is transformed in art ... Even the 'admiration and deeper feelings' with which the company regards the painting ... are signs that the experience has been removed from practical reality into a past that can now be safely admired and that brings satisfying feelings to the breast.''

5 See Hugh Trevor-Roper, ''The Invention of Tradition: The Highland Tradition of Scotland,'' in Eric Hobsbawm, ed., *The Invention of Tradition* (Cambridge: Cambridge University Press, 1983), pp. 15–16. Trevor-Roper argues that ''the whole concept of a distinct Highland culture and tradition is a retrospective invention.'' The Highlanders of Scotland were basically an overflow from Ireland. Until the mid-eighteenth century, when the West of Scotland was opened up during the Jacobite revolts, the Highlanders were racially and culturally Irish. Trevor-Roper divides ''the creation of an independent Highland tradition'' into three stages. Scott belongs to the third, when, after the cultural revolt against Ireland and the ''artificial creation of new Highland traditions,'' the ''new'' traditions were ''offered to, and adopted by, historic Lowland Scotland.''

6 Cf. Martin Green, *Dreams of Adventure, Deeds of Empire* (New York: Basic Books, 1979), pp. 102, 104–06. For Green, the larger political and intellectual context of Scott's writing is that crucial moment in European consciousness, described by Claude Lévi-Strauss in *Tristes Tropiques*, in which, as a consequence of the explorers' voyages, Europe was forced to perceive that it was not a complete and final entity, but part of a larger system, and that, to comprehend its own position, it must contemplate its new image in the mirror of alien cultures. Green also sees Scott as giving voice to ''an aristomilitary caste'' which was the dominant possessor of power in imperial England: ''Scott supplied a stream of rather fanciful images, rather obliquely related to reality, to the sons and daughters of that caste, and to those of the rest of the nation who admired them. Romantic, fanciful, merely historical as those images may seem, they gave a clearly satisfactory form and a fuller life to the aspirations of a large audience.''

7 Daiches, ''The Achievement of Walter Scott,'' p. 24.

8 On Scott's use of the picturesque, see Marcia Allentuck, ''Scott and the Picturesque: Afforestation and History,'' in Alan Bell, ed., *Scott Bicentenary Essays: Selected Papers Read at the Walter Scott Bicentenary*

Conference (New York: Barnes and Noble, 1973), pp. 193–94; and James Reed, *Walter Scott: Landscape and Locality* (London: Athlone Press, 1980), pp. 19–20.

9 See Hook's "Introduction" to the Penguin *Waverley* (New York: Penguin, 1971), p. 24, for his remarks on Scott's complicated attitude towards the picturesque in this passage.

10 See Robert C. Gordon, *Under Which King: A Study of the Scottish Waverley Novels* (Edinburgh and London: Oliver and Boyd, 1966), p. 17. Gordon offers a provocative, if somewhat casual, discussion of the role of sexual feeling in *Waverley* and in Scott's writing generally. He explains Waverley's "hopelessly stilted addresses" to Flora as a result of Scott's thorough diversion of "the power of Eros ... into a political channel."

11 See Lars Hartveit, *Dream Within a Dream: A Thematic Approach to Scott's Vision of Fictional Reality* (New York: Humanities Press, 1974), pp. 111–15, for an elaborate tracing out of the verbal links made by Scott between dreaming and the perceptions produced by Waverley's imaginative activity.

12 See Levine, *The Realistic Imagination*, p. 82: "... Scott indulges the excesses of romance which the hero must outgrow. What Edward Waverley must dismiss, *Waverley* preserves."

13 See Roland Barthes, "The Reality Effect," in Tzvetan Todorov, ed., *French Literary Theory Today* (Cambridge: Cambridge University Press, 1982), p. 11.

14 See Kenneth Sroka, "Scott's Aesthetic Parable: A Study of *Old Mortality*'s Two-Part Structure," *Essays in Literature*, 10 (2) (Fall 1983), pp. 183–97, and John B. Humma, "The Narrative Framing Apparatus of Scott's *Old Mortality*," *Studies in the Novel*, 12 (Winter 1980), pp. 301–15, on the novel's narrative structure.

15 In the Magnum Opus edition prepared by Scott in 1830, the author appended his own introduction to the other prefatory material. Cf. Jane Millgate, *Walter Scott*, pp. 47–61.

16 For background, see T. C. Smout's chapter, "The Working Class and the Radicals," in *A History of the Scottish People 1560–1830* (New York: Scribner's, 1969), pp. 440–48; William Ferguson's chapter, "The Struggle for Reform," in *Scotland: 1689 to the Present* (Edinburgh and London: Oliver and Boyd, 1968), pp. 266–90; and Gordon Donaldson, *Scotland: James I to James VII* (Edinburgh and London: Oliver and Boyd, 1965), pp. 367–73. See also Angus Calder, "Introduction" to *Old Mortality* (New York: Penguin, 1972), p. 10, for a brief, but valuable, discussion of Scott's attitude toward lower-class rebellion.

17 For reliable accounts of the historical and political context in which the wappen-schaw is supposed to have occurred, see Smout, *A History of*

the Scottish People, pp. 78–87, and Donaldson, *Scotland: James I to James VII*, pp. 358–84.

18 See, for instance, Brown, *Walter Scott and the Historical Imagination*, pp. 69–70: "For its encapsulation of an entire period with all its leading features and contradictions in one descriptive scene, the occasion of the wappen-schaw which opens the novel was probably never surpassed in Scott's work. Here, in the gathered array of crown vassals, and the reaction of the local tenants, Scottish society of the period stands symbolically displayed."

19 See Shaw, *The Forms of Historical Fiction*, p. 198, for a similar argument about this passage.

20 Cf. Welsh, *The Hero of the Waverley Novels*, p. 244.

21 Cf. Humma, "The Narrative Framing Apparatus of Scott's *Old Mortality*," p. 313: "We observe Henry, or we observe from Henry's perspective, because his consciousness is an extension of the sensitive Presbyterian Pattieson's. Henry's goals are Pattieson's goals, and his failures are tasted as sharply by Pattieson as by Henry himself. The tone of the story, then, continues and amplifies upon that of chapter one, Pattieson's introduction."

22 See, for example, Welsh, *The Hero of the Waverley Novels*, p. 256: "The conclusion of *Old Mortality* ... consists of a succession of extravagant scenes and stock situations that destroy the narrative illusion. The gratuitous promotion of the hero, his return as a wandering stranger, the unbelievable 'ghost' scene, the unspoken parallels to Odysseus, but also to Hamlet, the sudden introduction of a new villain, the patience of Evandale, fidelity of Edith, and the obliteration of Burley in a mist of Satanism and sublime nature are further weakened ... by the lapse of ten years which divide this rush of events from the main and superior part of the action ... *Old Mortality*, in short, succumbs to the stock material of fairy tales." These remarks may seem odd, coming as they do from a critic who approaches the Waverley novels as projective romances. But Welsh's remarks on the novel's final chapters are important for his acute observation of the ways in which the "fairy-tale" quality of the denouement militates against the realistic effect of the novel's main part.

23 Cf. Robert Gordon, *Under Which King*, p. 63. To Gordon, the ending of the novel implies Scott's "inability to envision a satisfactory synthesis of the strenuous antitheses of the Civil War."

24 Brown, *Walter Scott and the Historical Imagination*, pp. 88, 91, claims that in these last eight chapters, Scott "falls back on the hackneyed romance tradition," that these chapters "stand at the opposite pole from the brilliantly particularized scenes in the main part" of *Old Mortality*. Brown explains the difficulties of the ending as a result of the novel's

limited "Scottish focus." He argues that Scott tries to explain the Glorious Revolution in the same terms as the Whig revolt of 1679. But to "properly explain the events of 1688, a Scottish focus is not sufficient: this is Scott's fundamental difficulty in *Old Mortality* ... Though the settlement of 1689 was extremely favorable to the growth of the Scottish middle class ... it occurred for reasons outside the Scottish arena." Whatever the merits of Brown's historical argument may be, he errs in treating Scott as a historian *manqué*.

25 Cf. Sroka, "Scott's Aesthetic Parable: A Study of *Old Mortality*'s Two-Part Structure," p. 185: "... in *Old Mortality*'s form, Scott reenacts in the present of the reader the process by which a historical novel reveals the related but unique natures of historical and fictional composition. The reader experiences two verbal worlds, one predominantly but not exclusively 'historical,' the other predominantly but not exclusively 'fictional.' The novel's two-part structure reminds the reader in a work of fiction − as in a parable − of the paradoxical roles of history and fiction as complementary but independent."

26 See Welsh, *The Hero of the Waverley Novels*, p. 264: "The Waverley novels are romance ... the kind of fiction that projects a moral and dreamlike arrangement of things ..." In these last eight chapters, Scott sets out to write a "moral and dreamlike arrangement" of events against the gloomy prospect of Morton's exile with which the main part of the novel closes.

3 HISTORICAL FABLE AND POLITICAL FANTASY: *THE HEART OF MIDLOTHIAN* AND *THE BRIDE OF LAMMERMOOR*

1 The *Edinburgh Waverley* edition of the novel is published in the form of fifty-two consecutive chapters, as are most reprints. As first published in 1818, however, the novel was divided into four volumes. In the Riverside Edition (Boston: Houghton Mifflin Company, 1966), p. v, John Henry Raleigh describes his collation of the 1818 edition with the 1830 edition, arguing for the use of the first edition on the grounds that it is the most aesthetically coherent version of the novel: "Each volume ... is concerned with a well-defined portion of the whole story, and each has its own dramatic unity, rising to a climax at or near the end of the volume. In turn, the end of each volume has a twofold function: it concludes one section of the narrative and looks forward to the next." Despite Raleigh's good intentions, his reprint only serves to emphasize the generic disparity that has so often been observed by less sympathetic readers. This disparity has long been the focus of critical dissatisfaction with the novel. See Millgate, *Walter Scott: The Making of the Novelist*, p. 163. Millgate

defines the problem with the fourth volume as an inapt choice of representational technique: "Scott seeks to bring off the transition from historical narrative to political emblem by a fully orchestrated shift of mode – by projecting the Knocktarlitie episode as a pastoral expressive of Jeanie's attainment of a restored but transformed harmony, and by associating that harmony with the idea of Union ... But the specifically historical problems prove not to be readily susceptible of the technical solution provided by the move into the pastoral." See also Shaw, *The Forms of Historical Fiction*, p. 242: "The relevance of the fourth volume" is "the most problematic aspect of form in the novel." Allowing a partial legitimacy to critical complaints about the fourth volume, Shaw explains that Scott was concerned there with exploring the theme of "cultural transition," a theme derived from, but not expressly treated in, the novel's central action: "... hence, it naturally enough has always seemed somewhat extraneous to readers who believe, as they should, that Jeanie's action is the heart of the novel." Gordon, *Under Which King*, p. 94, views the chapters that follow Jeanie's interview with the Queen as "a disaster which reveals perhaps as nothing else in the Waverley novels Scott's capacity for an infantile disregard of aesthetic decencies." In a catalogue of grievances against *Midlothian*, Dorothy Van Ghent, in *The English Novel: Form and Function* (New York: Holt, Rinehart and Winston, 1961), pp. 114–15, observes: "We cannot cut short *The Heart of Midlothian* at that point where its older readers found it still so highly praiseworthy – the point where Jeanie obtains the pardon; we must judge the book at its full length without commiseration for Scott's financial needs in building Abbotsford." See Avrom Fleishman, *The English Historical Novel: Walter Scott to Virginia Woolf* (Baltimore and London: Johns Hopkins University Press, 1971), pp. 93–94, for the most plausible defense of the fourth volume, his claim that it is closely linked with the broader ethical transformation in which Jeanie is made over from a heroine of justice to a heroine of mercy.

2 See Thomas Crawford, *Sir Walter Scott* (Scottish Writers Series, Edinburgh: Scottish Academic Press, 1982), p. 96. Citing the work of the historian Eric Cregeen, Crawford regards the Roseneath episodes as an essentially accurate depiction of the conditions on the Duke's estate. But Crawford's argument ignores the fictionality deliberately asserted in Scott's announcement of his shift in technique and the flagrant stylization of such figures as Duncan of Knockdunder and Donacha du na Dunaigh.

3 See Welsh, *The Hero of the Waverley Novels*, p. 93, for his discussion of the idea of property in the Waverley novels.

4 Millgate, *Walter Scott*, pp. 152–53, usefully emphasizes the ways in which *Midlothian* reverses some of the key formal patterns of *Waverley* – Scott's

choice of a lower-class protagonist, the change in the direction of the protagonist from Scotland to England, and the novel's persistent marginalizing of characters of "romantic sensibility," most notably Staunton. Of the changes in Scott's protagonists from *Waverley* to *Midlothian*, Millgate observes that "the role-playing and costume-changing that were harmless episodes in the growth of Edward Waverley and some of Scott's other young heroes become ... dangerous signs of instability and failure of moral integrity."

5 Cf. Fleishman, *The English Historical Novel*, p. 93: "... despite the widely held view that the fourth volume ... is an unnecessary appendage, when Jeanie completes her career at Roseneath the novel comes full circle geographically and resolves its historical and ethical themes."

6 See Van Ghent, *The English Novel*, pp. 114, 116, 120. Van Ghent regards *Midlothian* as the product of an "incoherent world view" of which the most noteworthy element is Scott's treatment of Jeanie Deans's moral dilemma. But this "pivotal moral problem" is itself "infected with the general fault of confusion." The greatest weakness of the novel is that, instead of concentrating on the great issues of truth and falsehood which are raised in the study of Jeanie Deans, Scott deflects the reader's view to "highwaymen and kidnapping and queens and colorful eccentrics."

7 Cf. Wilt, *Secret Leaves*, p. 137. Wilt regards Jeanie as a figure of romance in the tradition of Edward Waverley whose ordeal is a "grappling with the real." Jeanie has undertaken her romance in the form of a Pilgrim's Progress. In her journey to the "earthly city" sought by Waverley pilgrims, she undergoes "an education in the uses of fictions, of mental reservation and canny speechlessness, of lies." Jeanie does, of course, dissemble. But it is the force of her language, of speech direct from the heart, which wins Effie's pardon, and not her ability to use fictions.

8 See Shaw, *The Forms of Historical Fiction*, pp. 234–38, for a concise description of the novel's formal and thematic inconsistencies, especially his discussions of the early chapters on the Porteous riots and the function of the Gothic figure of Staunton within the context of Scott's realistic intentions.

9 Cf. Crawford, *Sir Walter Scott*, p. 97. Crawford retracts his earlier judgment of the fourth volume: "... I was wrong when I wrote in 1965 that 'the tale degenerates toward yet another version of pastoral.'" For Crawford, Roseneath is not merely a way of patching over the novel's formal problems, but a "counter in what has, in the book's progress, become a historical fable. *The Heart of Midlothian* celebrates what was attained in the course of a long revolution, at the same time as it shows some (though insufficient) awareness of the price paid." Crawford is right to suggest that *Midlothian* has become a

"historical fable." But Roseneath is the culmination of that "fable," rather than a momentary reversal.

10 See Arnold Kettle, *Introduction to the English Novel* (New York: Oxford University Press, 1960), p. 111: "The Edinburgh section as well as being the longest is by far the best. Real issues, real people, real conflicts form it ... Scott's Edinburgh is not just a casual dwelling centre, but a Scottish city, unified by its Scottish consciousness, set in history so that the very title of the book, *The Heart of Midlothian*, comes to have a rich ambiguity which refers not merely to the place of execution, but to Edinburgh itself, the heart of Scotland." Taken as a description of Scott's conscious intentions in the Edinburgh section, Kettle's account is essentially accurate. But his praise of Scott as a truthful depictor of history strikes me as naive.

11 Cf. Gordon, *Under Which King*, p. 97. Gordon claims that *Midlothian* "marks the appearance in the Waverley novels of a deeply felt, almost desperate royalism." Cf. also Daniel Cottom, *The Civilized Imagination*, pp. 185–86. Cottom argues that Scott's preoccupation with weak or irresponsible rulers in *Midlothian* and in several other of his novels "is directed not to the constitutional or legal authority of monarchs but rather to their personal authority and power over the regulation of civil affairs ... For Scott, the monarch is, in effect, the spirit of the laws – the inspiring presence that is supposed to settle all disputes over the interpretation of the laws – and yet these novels do not display any great confidence in finding such a man of spirit. Scott's view of kings and queens and great lords and ladies is always an ironic one."

12 Cf. Shaw, *The Forms of Historical Fiction*, p. 237. Shaw regards Scott's use of Staunton as part of a "sustained attack on genteel expectations throughout the novel." Staunton and Effie are meant to embody "genteel" or "modern" assumptions about the value of "passionate interiority and individualism, as well as a certain escapism from the complexities of historical existence." Although Shaw's assumptions about the tastes of Scott's reading public are debatable, his estimation of Scott's ideological investment in Staunton and Effie seems to me essentially right.

13 See Millgate, *Walter Scott*, pp. 152–53, for her remarks on the altered value in *Midlothian* of "romantic sensibility" and "imaginative responsiveness."

14 See Fleishman, *The English Historical Novel*, p. 95. Citing Scott's "Essay on Chivalry," Fleishman argues that Staunton's career illustrates the tendency of chivalric ideals "to fall into their opposites: courtly love into licentiousness, freedom into turmoil, gallantry into mannered absurdity." Fleishman's reading renders Staunton as one of those familiar anachronisms who often have significant roles in the Waverley novels, the dispossessed feudal hero. But by implication such a reading exaggerates

the progressive aspects of Scott's political vision and deemphasizes the defensive thrust of Scott's ideology, the conservatism that makes outcasts of Staunton and Effie.

15 See Kettle, *Introduction to the English Novel*, p.105. Kettle finds in *Midlothian* an ideological shift from the "point of view of the peasantry" to that of the "paternalist landowner." Scott's ability to see his subject from below, as it were, is what gives the novel "its solid sense of real life and real issues ..." But Kettle misses the crucial point that Jeanie is not a peasant woman, but a fictive treatment of the peasantry by an Edinburgh Tory closely linked with the deluded class which he labels "paternalist landowners."

16 See Robin Mayhead, *Walter Scott* (Cambridge: Cambridge University Press, 1973), pp.44–66. For a discussion of the themes of "justice" and "mercy" in the novel, see A.O.J. Cockshut, *The Achievement of Walter Scott* (London: Collins, 1969), pp.171–92.

17 Shaw, *Forms of Historical Fiction*, p.239.

18 See Fleishman, *The English Historical Novel*, p.96: "The Roseneath scenes do not provide images of bounty alone, and the fourth volume – which has been scorned as a fatuous idyll – instead incurs the danger of dissipating its symbolic force by its realistic qualifications ... To end on the note of a Highland Arcadia would have been to create an apocalyptic realm outside of history: to add the Captain of Knockdunder and the Whistler is to bring that realm into the world of politics, crime, and the continued historical experience of Scotland." I share Fleishman's "faith that [Scott] knew what he was about" in the final chapters (*English Historical Novel*, p.96). But while any admirer of *Midlothian* must appreciate Fleishman's effort to defend the Knocktarlitie episodes as a continuation of Scott's realism, his explanation ignores the modal incongruities which make the final chapters the source of so much negative comment. It is precisely here that Fleishman's insistence on Scott's commitment to real history is most misleading.

19 See Cockshut, *The Achievement of Walter Scott*, p.85; and Brown, *Walter Scott and the Historical Imagination*, p.136. These critics explain the modal mixture of *The Bride* by arguing that its formal tensions are merely superficial and that the novel must be read as an essentially accurate account of the decline of the Scottish feudal aristocracy, combined with a rendering of the process from the perspective of the feudal consciousness.

20 See Eagleton, *Criticism and Ideology*, pp.70–91, for the conceptual framework of my discussion, especially the emphasis on the novel's formal contradictions. See Fredric Jameson's notion of "political fantasy" in *The Political Unconscious*, p.48.

21 Welsh, *The Hero of the Waverley Novels*, p.93.

22 See Eagleton, *Criticism and Ideology*, pp. 90–91, for his adaptation of the Freudian interpretative metaphor. Eagleton compares the work of the critic to that of the analyst as described in Freud's *The Interpretation of Dreams*. Extending the dream analogy, we can see the novel as a wish-fulfilling structure. *The Bride* can be regarded as embodying an act of desire, a vehicle for the expression of deep wishes emanating from a political unconscious of which Scott is a representative figure.

23 See Punter, *The Literature of Terror*, pp. 402–26, especially pp. 414–19, for his theory of the Gothic.

24 Punter, *The Literature of Terror*, p. 418.

25 Cf. Cottom, *The Civilized Imagination*, pp. 148–49. Cottom regards this passage as typical in its drawing of "a didactic line between the interest one may legitimately take in dramatic or marvelous events and the disgust one must feel at the surrender of self-control." Cottom argues that the supernatural in Scott's fiction is "a realm primarily distinguished from that of ordinary events by the fact that it strips individuals of power over themselves. It transforms individuals from responsible masters of themselves into irresponsible servants of forces foreign to their understanding." Cottom sees at work in this passage the "psychologizing of the supernatural." In such passages as these throughout Scott's fiction, this psychologizing is used "as a tool to enforce moral orthodoxy."

26 See Leo Bersani, *A Future for Astyanax: Character and Desire in Literature* (Boston: Little, Brown and Company, 1969), p. 67. Bersani argues forcefully that "Realistic fiction admits heroes of desire in order to submit them to ceremonies of expulsion."

27 Levine, *Realistic Imagination*, p. 113. Levine regards this as a key moment in the novel's larger process of domestication, a procedure which he describes as one of "translating the mysterious and monstrous into entirely human terms" (p. 120).

28 For background, see William Ferguson, *Scotland: 1689 to the Present* (Edinburgh and London: Oliver & Boyd, 1968), pp. 88–185; and I. F. Grant, *The Economic History of Scotland* (London: Longman's, Green, and Co., 1934), pp. 159–202. Even before the Union in 1701, the landed aristocracy of Scotland was closely tied with the commercial interests which are often cited as the target of the novel's social and moral critique. By the time of the Union, the Scottish nobility and gentry, through their investments in coalmining, the cattle trade, and the linen trade were heavily dependent on exports to England for their income. This reliance on exports necessitated close ties between the landed classes and the merchants of Scotland and England. Despite the loss of political independence legislated in the Union, the opening of English markets to Scottish exports had no small appeal to the Scottish aristocracy.

29 See Shaw, *The Forms of Historical Fiction*, pp. 215–16. Shaw's skillful use of biographical material, particularly his treatment of the linkage between sexual feelings and class loyalties in the novel, helps to explain the modal tensions and thematic disjunctions which pervade *The Bride*. For a succinct account of the Belsches affair, see Johnson, *Sir Walter Scott: The Great Unknown*, pp. 108–124.

30 See Terry Eagleton, *Criticism and Ideology*, p. 70. I am indebted again to Eagleton for the terms of my discussion here.

4 *REDGAUNTLET*: THE HISTORICAL ROMANCE AS METAFICTION

1 Scott appended an "Introduction" to the Magnum Opus edition of *Old Mortality* which was printed in 1830, thereby adding a layer to the work of Jedidiah Cleisbotham and Peter Pattieson. Scott's story of his own encounter with Old Mortality lends a certain credence to Peter Pattieson's claims of objectivity; it serves as an authorial endorsement of Pattieson's editorial efforts against the dismissals of Cleisbotham.

2 See Walter Reed, *An Exemplary History of the Novel* (Chicago: University of Chicago Press, 1981), pp. 267, 271. Reed regards the tension described here as a definitive feature of the novel throughout its history: "Novels play 'literature' and 'history' off against one another as codified forms of written discourse. They reopen poetic closures by appealing to the more random plots of supposed historical phenomena. But they also foreclose historical reference. They betray the surviving records of the past to the logics of literary coherence – the logics of plot, of character, of point of view, and of their more particular protocols of narration." As Reed goes on to argue, "The term 'historical novel' is, then, something of a redundancy, comparable to the redundancy of 'nouveau roman': a local or specific reaffirmation of a proposition inherent in the novel from its beginnings." If all novels are historical, then the "historical novel" as conceived by Scott, widely considered a secondary genre, deserves a more prominent place in histories of the novel. Scott's overtly "historical" novels not only reflect an "inherent proposition" of the novel, but render the tension between "literature" and "history" as an inescapable dilemma for the writer who would represent the past. Scott's fiction, I believe, represents an important self-reflexive moment in the history of the novel.

3 See Brian Nellist, "Narrative Modes in the Waverley Novels," in R. T. Davies and R. G. Beatty, eds., *Literature of the Romantic Period, 1750–1850* (Liverpool: Liverpool University Press, 1976), pp. 56–71,

especially pp. 57–59. Nellist describes the modal mixture of the Waverley novels as a play of voices: "What we hear continually in the Waverley Novels ... is a dialogue between the claims of two literary modes. These modes, proposed by eighteenth-century criticism, are the romance and the novel." For Nellist, "romance" and "novel" are cultural distinctions, as well as literary terms: "Through the historical medium, the viewpoints of romance and novel become images of rival cultures which have themselves created the consciousness of the artist. Scott, like his wavering heroes, is a solitary who knows he does not belong in romance and feels he does not want to belong in the novel."

4 See Miriam Allott, ed., *Novelists on the Novel*, p. 49.

5 F. R. Hart, *Scott's Novels: The Plotting of Historic Survival* (Charlottesville: University of Virginia Press, 1966), p. 52.

6 See Hart, *Scott's Novels*, p. 50. Hart argues that Joshua is "the chief exponent of the novel's governing values," and that Scott intended for us to accept at face value the Quaker's professed devotion to "plainspeaking."

7 See Coleman Parsons, *Witchcraft and Demonology in Scott's Fiction* (Edinburgh and London: Oliver and Boyd, 1964), p. 182, on Scott's use of traditional sources for "Wandering Willie's Tale."

8 See Fleishman, *The English Historical Novel*, p. 73. Emphasizing Scott's "philosophical" tendencies, Fleishman claims that "The Tale resumes the sequence of stages by which a typical feudal family is seen moving, after the Glorious Revolution, from feudal indolence to economically pinched hardness, and finally to temperate adherence to the new order of modern life." But this kind of reading focuses on one facet of the tale, setting aside its anti-realistic elements – its frame within Darsie's letter, its supernatural elements, the narrator's reputation as a taleteller. To make a point which is, perhaps, all too obvious, the tale may very well be a reflection of Scott's "philosophical" historicism. But it is also a narrative, a story about the past, which can accommodate several disparate interpretations.

9 Cf. Margaret Cullinan, "History and Language in Scott's *Redgauntlet*," *Studies in English Literature*, 18 (1978), p. 667. Cullinan argues that the tale, "while primarily a legend recounting the story of a visit to Hell ... is constructed so that there are possible realistic explanations to the events; we can never decide what aspects of the tale are entirely fictional."

10 Cf. Nellist, "Narrative Modes in the Waverley Novels," p. 69. Nellist finds in *Redgauntlet* a unity that "transcends" the opposition of romance and novelistic perspectives: "Its true center is the narrator's own consciousness, admitting all, ironic, tragic, humorous, always observant – the fictional viewpoint." The "fictional viewpoint" is implicit in Scott's

techniques of fabulation, but not in the "consciousness" of the narrator. The narrator in *Redgauntlet*, despite the congenial voice, is clearly to be considered as a device of the author, and not as a character. The novel's unity is a result of Scott's shift away from depicting history towards reflecting on the theoretical issues he had first raised in *Waverley* and *Old Mortality*.

INDEX